The Last Phase in the Transformation of Capitalism

The Last Phase in the Transformation of Capitalism

Michal Kalecki

Introduction by
George R Feiwel

Preface by
Wxodzimierz Brus

The Last Phase in the Transformation of Capitalism
Michal Kalecki

First Published in India 2011
Reprinted 2023

ISBN 978-93-5002-143-9

Published in arrangement with Monthly Review Press, New York for publication and sale in South Asia only.

Published by
AAKAR BOOKS
28 E Pocket IV, Mayur Vihar Phase I
Delhi 110 091, India
www.aakarbooks.com

Printed at
D.K. Fine Art Press, Delhi

Contents

Introduction: Notes on the Life and Work of Michal Kalecki

by George R. Feiwel

In the field of economics, or more broadly in the social sciences, there are few who can claim to have had an impact on changing the course of science. One such man in our own lifetime was Professor Michal Kalecki, who died on April 17, 1970, in Warsaw, at the age of 71. He not only anticipated the "Keynesian revolution" in economics and contributed vastly to the theoretical foundations and explanation of modern capitalism in motion, but he also made a lasting and monumental contribution to the theory of economic growth under socialism, achieved a breakthrough in perspective economic planning and in planning methodology in general, contributed significantly to the measurement of efficiency of investments and foreign trade, and advanced research on the problems of

I am indebted to Joan Robinson for reviewing and improving a part of this paper. I have also benefited from discussions with Maurice Dobb, Alexander Erlich, Mario Nuti, George Shackle, Piero Sraffa, and Paolo Sylos-Labini. Of course, I alone shoulder all responsibility.

industrializing developing nations. The range of Kalecki's interests embraces the economics of capitalist, socialist, and mixed economies.

But Kalecki was never satisfied with merely providing a theoretical explanation and an analytical toolbox. He considered it his duty to influence events—to participate actively in shaping economic policy in his own country and abroad. These efforts were probably a source of many disappointments, irritations, and lost energy; the logic of economic arguments, no matter how ironclad, does not usually prevail in adopting economic policy. Original and creative economic advisors often lead a lonely life. One of the paradoxes of history seems to be that in a socialist economy, where the state is invested with the power to shape the direction of the economy and where there is insignificant reliance on the so-called feedback-mechanism of the market, the role of the economist in making economic policy decisions is inconsequential.

Apart from his involvement in advising the Polish planners, Michal Kalecki was postwar economic advisor to the Israeli, Cuban, and Indian governments. He once remarked ironically that his only immediate impact was a negative correlation, in the case of Israel, where the policies adopted were the exact opposite of those he had recommended. An indication of Kalecki's remarkable ability to grasp economic problems and to identify priorities is his advice that Cuba should not endeavor to develop a steel industry, but that as an immediate task it should build a plant to manufacture spare parts for imported machinery, with the dual effect that the bottlenecks would be widened more rapidly and that the domestic labor force would be trained in the process.

I

We can only skim here the surface of the Keynesian revolution in economics and of Kalecki's unique role in it. Prior to this breakthrough, the classical theory that dominated economic thought and policy viewed the capitalist economy as a natural, self-propelled, and self-regulating mechanism ("supply creates its own demand"), in which a tendency to establish full employment prevails. Such an economy tends to maintain full employment, and unemployment may be considered as merely an accidental, temporary displacement and deviation from full utilization of economic resources—a rather unimportant frictional occurrence which may largely be disregarded. The flexibility of wages and prices ensures the mechanism. Unemployment may be cured by reducing money wages, since employment will rise with a decline of real wages. Unemployed workers, competing for employment, will be willing to lower the price for their labor. The wage reduction, by making labor relatively cheaper, should induce substitution of labor for other factors, thereby increasing employment. (Rigid prices and institutional factors, such as trade unions, may obstruct the equilibrating process by artificially maintaining wages.) *Ceteris paribus,* should wages be appropriately reduced the unemployed, willing to accept a cut in wages, would find employment. Wages would fall more rapidly than prices. Profit margins would be improved. But wages have both cost and income effects. The reduction of money wages, *inter alia,* reduces money income and effective demand.

The classicists considered the rate of interest another device for equilibrating savings and investment. Since the alternative to consumption is savings (income not consumed), a decline in consumers' expenditures increases savings. With a larger volume of savings, the savers compete to earn the highest terms. Unable to find borrowers at the prevailing rate, the savers lower their rates. At the lower rewards, some savers are discouraged and choose to consume. At the same time, investors are encouraged to invest more and to employ a larger volume of savings since at lower borrowing rates the previously unprofitable investment ventures may become profitable. Thus employment, in producing both consumption and investment goods, is expanded.

As modern macroeconomic theory has shown, an *ex ante* increase of non-spending on consumption (savings) does not guarantee additional investments. Equally, an *ex ante* rise in savings is not a prerequisite for additional investment. The decision to invest is independent of the decision to save. While the former is, *inter alia,* governed by the businessman's anticipation of profit, the latter is mainly a function of income. There is no mechanism to ensure that investment will increase so as to fill the gap for the deficiency of effective demand. Moreover, a decline of consumption expenditures reduces derived demand for additional equipment required for the production of goods. As a result of a decrease of consumption, the businessman's revenue drops. Part of the product produced will remain unsold and inventories of goods will thus pile up. Losses permeate the system. Output will be cut down and businessmen will reduce their labor force. With growing unemployment, income declines. With a fall in income, savings are reduced. Should the volume of investment remain stationary, income will decline to the point where, at the lower income, the reduced savings will equal investment. The equilibrating mechanism takes place through the variation of income rather than through the rate of interest.

Michal Kalecki earned his first claim to immortality by anticipating the "Keynesian revolution" from which modern macroeconomic theory evolved. In more technical terms, the "Keynesian revolution"

> may be summarized in the propositions that the rate of saving is governed by the rate of investment, that the level of prices is governed by the level of money wage rates, and that the level of interest rates is governed by the supply and demand of money.[1]

The "Keynesian revolution" refers, *inter alia,*[2] to the impact of the theory of determination and fluctuations of the level of aggregate output and employment, underscoring the dependence and impact of the level and structure of effective demand on the level of economic activity and on the degree of utilization of labor and productive capacity, emphasizing that fluctuations in the volume of investment will cause and be accompanied by corresponding fluctuations in economic activity, expenditures, output, incomes, and employment. The policy, implicit in the theory, assigns a crucial role to deliberate government policy as an instrument for regulating or influencing effective demands: in case of deficiency of demand, by filling the gap between total income generated and private expenditures on consumption, capital formation, and net exports through compensatory fiscal policy, government expenditures to increase (or to reduce, in case of deficiency of productive capacities) the volume of expenditures.

The role of investment in establishing a certain level of national product is not associated with the final destination or the uses to which the investment will eventually be put. It is its income-generating effect that matters at the time when it is carried out. Whether the investment will prove to be useful or useless in the future is inconsequential from the standpoint of the equilibrating process of current (short-run) macroeconomic equilibrium. What matters is its role from the standpoint of the equilibrating process: that it generates the same effective demand when it is executed. It follows that from the standpoint of creating effective demand it is inconsequential, ruling out offsetting effects, whether private investments are replaced by government expenditures, financed by loans—to mention here only one policy alternative—so that no reduction of any purchasing power by taxation is involved. By means of what Kalecki calls "financial tricks" (fiscal weapons, functional finance), the government expenditures, financed by budget deficits, can solve the insufficiency of effective demand; and, if they are appropriately large, they can ensure full employment. If the aim is to restore full employment, as far as the generation of effective demand is concerned the direction of government expenditures is largely immaterial (perhaps given some appropriate assumption as to the propensity to consume). When investments fall short of savings, or of that level which is necessary to maintain effective demand, it is the basis of government policies in modern capitalism that the gap is governed by government expenditures (or taxes are reduced so as to increase disposable income and expenditures on consumption, and measures are taken to induce investments).

Keynes's monumental *General Theory of Employment, Interest, and Money* was published in 1936. In 1933, outside of the mainstream of traditional economic theory, an unknown Polish economist, without formal training in economics, brought up almost exclusively on Marx[3] and influenced by the writings of Rosa Luxemburg,[4] without any contact with Keynes,

> created a system that contains everything of importance in the Keynesian system, in addition to other contributions . . . [Kalecki] has a theory of employment that is the equal of Keynes's . . . he certainly lacked Keynes's reputation or ability to draw world-wide attention; hence his achievement is relatively unnoticed.[5]

When Kalecki was visiting Sweden in 1936 he began dictating to his wife what would have constituted a comprehensive treatise on the main ideas he had developed. He then learned of the publication of Keynes's *General Theory*. When he read the book he discovered that it contained most of what he had wanted to say.[6] He immediately interrupted his work and left for England where he contacted the Keynesians and was soon considered an exponent of Keynes's theories.[7] With his usual modesty Kalecki never told Keynes that he had a prior claim on "his" theory. While Keynes expounded to Kalecki that hardly anyone over the age of forty understood Newton's theory, thus drawing a parallel to the lack of understanding Keynes's own theories were meeting, Kalecki was far too modest even to assume such a comparison. Kalecki's anticipation of the *General Theory* has only been publicly recognized since Keynes's death. However, he never regretted his retiring attitude during those years and recently commented that he would not have acted differently with hindsight. For,

> as Michal Kalecki is the first to admit, the "Keynesian Revolution" in Western academic economics is rightly so called. For without Keynes' wide sweep, his brilliant polemic, and, above all, his position within the orthodox citadel, in which he was brought up, the walls of obscurantism would have taken much longer to break.[8]

The record was finally set straight by one of Keynes's most distinguished students, Joan Robinson, who with her own "proper scholarly dignity," attested that:

> Michal Kalecki's claim to priority of publication is indisputable. With proper scholarly dignity (which, however, is unfortunately rather rare among scholars) he never mentioned this fact. And, indeed, except for the authors concerned, it is not particularly interesting to know who first got into print. The interesting thing is that two thinkers, from completely different political and intellectual starting points, should come to the same conclusion. For us in Cambridge it was a great comfort. Surrounded by blank misunderstanding, there were moments when we almost began to wonder if it were we who were mad or the others. In the serious sciences, original work is *discovery*—finding connections that were always there, waiting to be seen. That this could happen in economics was a reassurance that what we had discovered was really there.[9]

Kalecki's original (1933) essay on the business cycle theory withstood the test of time and great transformations in economics.[10] In an introduction to an English translation, published for the first time in 1966, Joan Robinson wrote: "Its sharp and concentrated statement provides a better introduction to the general theory of employment, interest and money than any that has yet been produced." [11]

It is noteworthy that in some respects Kalecki's model is superior to that of Keynes. Namely, "it is explicitly dynamic; it takes income distribution as well as level into account; and it makes the important distinction between investment orders and investment outlays." [12] On the one hand, Kalecki did not approach the theory of macroeconomic equilibrium and employment through the multiplier effect—a major contribution to economics by a

brilliant student of Keynes's, Professor (now Lord) Kahn,[13] "which makes his version in a way less rich than Keynes', though no less forceful. On the other hand, he went straight to the theory of the trade cycle, on which Keynes was very weak." [14] Whereas Keynes's theory was couched in terms of a closed system, Kalecki extended his analysis to the crucial repercussions of the balance of payments.[15] Another aspect that can only be mentioned in passing is the political divergency between Kalecki and Keynes. Whereas the latter was primarily a reformer of capitalism, the former was an advocate of socialism. It should also be noted that in a later work,[16] Kalecki modified principally the analysis of the determinants of investment decisions and allowed for alterations in stockbuilding during the course of the business cycle.[17]

In the Foreword to the English edition of *Studies in the Theory of Business Cycles, 1933–1939,* Kalecki reflected that the development of his theory as presented in the *Theory of Economic Dynamics* (1954),

> which was quite laborious, hardly earned me any applause. It was frequently maintained that the first version was more lucid and elegant. I myself consider that the modifications introduced meant some progress since the later version of the theory seems to me better founded and more realistic.[18]

While Keynes did not pay much attention to price theory, Kalecki incorporated into his analysis both the theory of individual prices (distribution) and effective demand (employment) by demonstrating that the determination of gross profit margin is cardinal to the distribution of the value added in industry between wage earners and capitalists and, therefore, conditions effective demand and employment.[19]

Kalecki has made seminal contributions to the theory of

economic dynamics.[20] One of the leading econometricians of our time, L. R. Klein, attested that the econometric models he has constructed as practical tools for analyzing and forecasting the United States, Canadian, British, and Japanese economies have been based on combinations from the theoretical macroeconomic models of Marx, Kalecki, Keynes, Lange, Hicks, Kaldor, Metzler, Goodwin, and others. While it is customary to attribute the recent upsurge of macroeconomic model-building in the modern econometric systems as an outgrowth of the neo-Keynesian development, *de facto* most macroeconomic models presently in existence "could be decomposed into ideas first found in the models of Kalecki, Kaldor, Metzler, and Goodwin. The latter three could have been developed as natural extensions of the Kalecki theory." [21] Klein acknowledged that

> it can be said that all the components of Kalecki's model are finding their way into strategic places in modern econometric models. His theories of the early 1930's are seen to be intellectual *tours de force* in the light of modern developments.[22]

II

Marx was deeply aware of the impact of effective demand on the dynamics of the capitalist economy,[23] but he did not systematically scrutinize the process described in his reproduction scheme from the standpoint of the "inherent contradictions of the capitalist economy" as a result of the problem of effective demand.[24]

Marx's follower Rosa Luxemburg rejected altogether the possibility of a long-term expanded reproduction in "a closed capitalist system." She maintained that the development of capitalism relied entirely on the existence of possible realization outlets outside the world capitalist system—the "external markets." The latter were composed not only of underdeveloped economies but also included the non-capitalist sectors of developed capitalist economies, such as peasant agriculture and the government sector. "Export" outside the sphere of capitalist sectors was considered by Luxemburg as the *spiritus novens* of development.

If Rosa Luxemburg unduly stressed the impossibility of the development of capitalist economies without "external markets" and disregarded some expansion due to certain aspects of technical progress, the significance of "external markets" for the development of capitalist economies cannot be dismissed. Kalecki argues that one of the most interesting elements of Luxemburg's theory relevant to present-day capitalism is the treatment of government purchases, especially of armaments, as a form of "external market," a market that plays a crucial role in the functioning of modern capitalism. True, Rosa Luxemburg did not treat these government expenditures as being of primary importance; nor did she envision the possibility of averting crises by the income effect that such expenditures generate. Moreover, as in the case of other "external markets" she committed the error of treating total government expenditures as a factor of realizing surplus production, i.e., independently of the means of financing. Government expenditures, to the extent that they are financed (not offset) by budgetary deficits or by taxation of capitalists, contribute to solving the problem of effective demand because their effect—in contrast to financing government expenditures by indirect or direct taxation of workers, who largely spend what they earn—contributes to solving the cardinal problem of effective demand, as their effect is not offset by the decline of investment and consumption expenditures.

While this is not the place to analyze Rosa Luxemburg's argument about "external markets," it may be noted in passing that one of the flaws in her reasoning was identification of investment decisions not with individual decisions of investors but with the capitalist class investing as a whole. This class, frustrated by the knowledge that in the end it will not be possible to realize the economic surplus, will see no reason to undertake such investments. In Kalecki's view, Luxemburg's skepticism as to the possibility of long-term expanded reproduction is valuable since the self-propelled growth of capitalist economies cannot be taken for granted. Expanded reproduction does not necessarily ensure long-trend satisfactory utilization of productive capacities. Kalecki maintains that despite Luxemburg's erroneous claim that the development of capitalism depends entirely on "external markets," the latter are essential factors in dynamics.[25]

Kalecki maintained that long-term growth of the national product, involving satisfactory utilization of productive capacity in a capitalist economy, is far from obvious,[26] *inter alia,* because the monopolistic factors involved in price fixing are deeply rooted in the capitalist mode of production, conditioning the relationships between wages and prices both during the course of business cycles and in the long run, and cannot be treated merely as temporary short-run price rigidities.

III

Whereas the crucial problem of a developed capitalist economy is the adequacy of effective demand, as such an economy possesses a stock of productive capital which more or less matches the existing labor force and is therefore capable of generating a rather high per capita income, provided that its resources are fully employed. The cardinal problem of the underdeveloped (or less developed) economies is the deficiency of productive capacity rather than the question of its variable utilization (underutilization).[27]

In the standard, essentially "short-run" and static Keynesian system,[28] investment is merely treated in its income-generating capacity, and the essential and fundamental properties of investment that create the additional productive capacity of the economy are not taken into account, no doubt in view of the problems that the author of the towering *General Theory* was tackling and the uses his analytical construct was aimed at.

In underdeveloped economies, even if the meager productive capital is fully utilized it is not of sufficient size to be capable of absorbing all available labor resources. Consequently, the standard of living persists at a very low level. This is not to deny that an underdeveloped country may suffer from a deficiency of effective demand and underutilization of even its meager capacities. But the core problem cannot be remedied by "financial tricks." Here the central issue is deficiency of productive capacity rather than the anomaly of its underemployment. The spotlight shifts from the problem of full utilization to how capacity could be considerably and rapidly enlarged, not for the sake of creating sufficient effective demand, but in order to accelerate the expansion of this capacity as a *conditio sine qua non* for a rapid rise in national income.

The increase of investment meets three essential obstacles: First, it is possible that private investment will not be forthcoming at a sufficiently high rate. Second, the economy may face a shortage of the natural resources and human skills necessary for increasing the production of investment goods. Third, even if the first two obstacles are overcome there still remains the problem of an adequate supply of necessities to satisfy the demand resulting from increased employment. In the case of the first obstacle, it is obvious that it is especially difficult in underdeveloped countries to reach a high level of private investment; but there is a possibility of supplementing private investments with state investments in order to reach the required level. In the case of the second obstacle, it can be assumed that certain reserves exist, especially in construction. Furthermore, a significant share of investment goods is obtained through indirect production. In such a situation, as soon as investment is increased inflationary pressures for necessities will be generated since their supply is limited. This difficulty cannot be overcome by financing additional investments through taxation of profits, for that would lead to a situation where profit after taxes will not rise and the capitalist consumption will not tend to increase. Because of higher employment there will be pressures on the limited supply of necessities and their prices will rise to a level where real wages of the enlarged wage bill will be equal to the unchanged supply of necessities. Profits before taxes will increase by the amount of additional investment, but this increment will be taxed away. Thus, both profits after taxes and the real wage bill will remain unchanged. However, with increased employment more work will be executed for the same real wages, i.e., real wages per worker will fall. Consequently, a higher level of investment will be possible. Kalecki argued that this would be a highly inequitable way of increasing investment to accelerate economic growth.

The intensity of these basic difficulties of underdeveloped economies can be significantly lessened if they are analyzed within the framework of a perspective plan, rather than as an abrupt acceleration of the expansion of productive capacities (take-off). In constructing such a plan both a gradual growth of investment in relation to national income and a gradual increase of the production of necessities can be taken into account. Inflationary pressures can be prevented by planning the increase of the supply of necessities to match the growth of demand for them resulting from the planned increase of national income.

Parallel to this, a second basic problem of the planned development of an underdeveloped economy consists of a gradual increase in investment in relation to national income. An increase in the share of investment is synonymous with a lowering of the share of consumption of the national product. Kalecki maintained that in order to achieve this end equitably luxuries should be taxed to restrict their consumption. Thus the gradual acceleration of the growth of national product will be accompanied by an increase in the supply of necessities adequate to prevent potent inflationary pressures. At the same time, a larger share of investment in national income will be compensated for by a reduction of the share of consumption of luxuries in national income, achieved through direct and indirect taxation of the wealthier segments of the population.

This theoretical solution to the problem of the non-inflationary growth of developing economies in practice meets with serious difficulties of a political nature. The first obstacle arises at the point of introducing the basic elements of a planned economy. Not only the size but also the structure of investment need to be planned since investment has to be properly allocated between production of necessities, non-essentials, and investment goods. This requires greater state intervention than that which aims at achieving full use of production capacities in the developed capitalist economies. On the one hand, the state must invest in all areas where private investment proves insufficient or unprofitable (external returns to investment), and, on the other, in activities where it would contravene desiderata.

The most difficult task is to ensure the adequate growth of necessities. Let us assume that investments are earmarked for agriculture and for industry producing fertilizers in order to ensure the output of a planned growth of foodstuffs. In an underdeveloped economy agricultural production meets with a series of constraints hampering its growth, even if agriculture were to dispose of all indispensable resources. These obstacles have their source in feudal, or semi-feudal, property relationships, in the system of land-lease, and in the domination of poor peasants by traders and money-lenders. Thus agricultural development cannot be accelerated without adequate institutional changes. An agrarian reform is by itself insufficient. The experience of many developing nations shows that, abstracting from the circumstances and manipulations of the reform, it does not solve the problem of the poor peasants' dependence on traders and money-lenders. Obviously it is much more difficult to overcome the opposition of privileged groups than, as in the case of the developed capitalist state, to introduce state financial intervention to solve the problems of deficiency of effective demand.

Finally, there remains the problem of taxation of privileged groups in order to finance increased investment. Taxation in underdeveloped economies is itself difficult and tax evasion is a common practice. This argument is often used by the privileged groups in combating tax regulations. As a result, no essential progress can be obtained in this area.

The three above-mentioned issues—state intervention in investment to ensure its planned size and structure, the overcoming of institutional barriers to a rapid development of agriculture, and an adequate taxation of the wealthy and better-to-do segments of the population—clearly present essentially political problems. In theory most ruling groups will agree and approve of the undertaking of such measures as an economic necessity. But when it comes to their implementation, undermining a whole gamut of privileges and vested interests, the situation changes radically and various forms of decisive opposition develop (indeed, one could add that the situation is similar to the opposition to economic reforms in the socialist economies).

IV

Whereas Kalecki's fame in the West probably rests mainly on his contributions to modern macroeconomics and to the development of dynamic theories, his contributions to the development of a theory of economic growth and planning under socialism and to the elaboration of a perspective plan will probably gain an equal place in the history of economic thought, and will become as important in influencing economic policy. Historical parallels are difficult and this is not the place to make conjectures on the likely impact of theories on policy.

Alfred Marshall once said that any short statement in economics must be wrong, with the possible exception of the present one. This definitely applies to any condensed presentation of Kalecki's austere and laconic exposition. We can only broadly trace Kalecki's contributions to the economics of socialism, without giving full justice to the richness of thought, to the magnificent logic of construction, and to the masterful development of the argument.

The "objective function" assumed in Kalecki's model of the socialist economy differs in *toto caelo* from that in his celebrated model of the capitalist economy. At the turn of the century a Russian economist, Tugan-Baranowsky, emphasized that the production of consumer goods does not constitute the "objective function" of the capitalist economy, nor does the demand for consumer goods constitute the propeller of the engine of economic development of the capitalist mode of production.[29] Tugan-Baranowsky's developed capitalism was a system in which machines are to produce machines to produce more machines, *ad infinitum,* assuming complete independence of capitalist development from the behavior of the market for consumer goods and with consumption becoming increasingly an expendable variable. Tugan-Baranowsky's answer to those critics who maintained that a system where investments are not earmarked for the production of consumer goods, but for machines, is irrational and absurd, was that the "objective function" of the capitalists is not fulfillment of consumers' wants but profit. In Kalecki's interpretation, granted the premises of the capitalist system, it is not at all absurd for expansion to rest on the growth of production of "iron and coal" which always serves the purpose of further expanding the production of "iron and coal." The production of "iron and coal" has "equal rights" with the production of "bread," provided that it is profitable. Consumption is the ultimate goal and criterion of a "harmonious," but not of an "antagonistic," system. The capitalist system is considered by Kalecki to be an antagonistic one whose purpose is to ensure profit for capital.

Kalecki emphatically stressed that the primary aim of the socialist economy is (or should be) consumption. He fought against the voluntaristic setting of inordinately ambitious growth rates and exposed the burdens of excessive investments and the impact of an adverse time distribution of consumption path. The non-fulfillment of an unrealistic plan reflects mainly, and in the final analysis, on current (short-run) consumption. Planners exhibit a natural penchant for maintaining the continuity of the investment processes in order to avoid extensive freezing of capital in unfinished projects. The recurring dramatic underfulfillments of consumption plans bear witness to it. Faced with an overambitious plan and built-in inefficiencies, the planner is prompt to compensate for blunders by reshuffling resources from consumption to priority targets. Kalecki forcefully argued against underestimating the damage caused by the underfulfillment of consumption plans. The apathy of the population which flows from this does not only have multifarious adverse consequences in economic life (it conditions the performance of the human agents of economic progress), but, what is no less important, it is negatively reflected in the socialist consciousness of society.

While one of the key problems of the capitalist economy is that of realization, the fundamental problems of the socialist economy are production, productivity, technical progress, techniques of production, volume and pattern of capital formation, investment efficiency, foreign trade and its efficiency, realistic and effective planning, equitable income distribution, etc.

In the socialist economy the question of realization is solved (or is capable of being solved) by planning authorities—by setting appropriate terms of exchange. Indeed, one of the principal superiorities of the socialist economy is—as Kalecki emphasized—that it can solve the focal question of effective demand simply by fixing the relative levels of prices and wages so as to ensure full utilization of resources, and can simultaneously resolve the problem of financing non-consumption expenditures (accumulation).

Kalecki formulated and applied to long-term planning certain basic growth relationships. He catalogued and analyzed certain essential constituent components and crucial factors governing and inhibiting the growth processes of the socialist economy, providing a framework for the analysis of the dynamics and barriers in the centrally planned economy.[30] He focused attention on three key factors which are singled out as the major determinants of change in Gross National Product:

1. The output effect or productivity of current gross productive investment commissioned during a year, expressed by the component $1/m \cdot I$, where m stands for the investment-output (incremental capital-output) ratio (i.e., the volume of additional investment required to produce an incremental unit of national product). The inverse of the investment-output ratio, $1/m$, denotes the productive (output) effect of investments, or efficiency of investment. *Ceteris paribus*, the volume of investment multiplied by the inverse of the investment-output ratio designates the incremental change in national product to which it conceptually gives rise, or to which it is attributed. The rate of change of gross national product $\left(r = \frac{\Delta Y}{Y}\right)$ yielded by gross capital formation equals the share of gross productive investments in gross national product $\left(i, \text{ where } i = \frac{I}{Y}\right)$ multiplied by the coefficient of investment efficiency ($1/m$). The behavior of $1/m$ depends chiefly on the nature and the prevailing type of technical and organizational prog-

ress (neutral, encouraging, or discouraging capital intensity), the states of labor supply (unlimited, limited reserves, full employment), endowment of natural resources, impact of foreign trade, and stage of economic development. The planner maximand is r (or Y). Y is defined as Gross Domestic (including so-called material services) Product (value added) in a given year in constant price valuations.

2. Kalecki focused attention on the rate of reduction of Y attributable to the annual replacement of worn-out plant or equipment. *Ceteris paribus,* the existing production capacity "shrinks" periodically, the parameter of amortization, a, denotes the (annual) rate of curtailment of the existing fixed productive capacities as a result of a retirement of capital goods of "old vintage." Consequently, Y declines (ΔY), owing to this capacity-reducing coefficient, by aY per unit of time (annum).

3. There is the coefficient of improvement, independent of investment, called the parameter of independent improvement, u. This *non-investment* source of periodical (annual)increment (or rather change) of Y results primarily from more effective utilization of existing capacities (such as increase of employment in existing plants and the number of shifts worked), reorganization of production processes, general changes in plan implementation and in the functioning of the planned economy, non-investment measures to eliminate the obstacles to a full utilization of existing productive potential, measures to alleviate disproportions of the various degrees of plan fulfillment resulting in "unbalancing" the material balances, widening of bottlenecks, mitigation of interruptions of inter-branch and inter-enterprise flows, economy in the use of materials, elimination of waste, decrease in work stoppages, improvements in the organization of work, refinement of employees' skills, etc. The annual contribution yielded by those

non-investment measures equals uY, where u stands for the coefficient of the effect of these improvements. The impact of gross investments, disinvestments, and non-investment growth determinants on change of Y can be summarized as:

$$\Delta Y = 1/m \cdot I - aY + uY$$

Because of a preoccupation with rates at which various economic quantities are changing over time, we get the proportional rate of growth of the aggregate volume of production, in what may be termed Kalecki's fundamental growth equation:

$$r = \frac{\Delta Y}{Y} = 1/m \cdot \frac{I}{Y} - a + u$$

With given appropriate assumptions as to the behavior of the non-investment variable and the rate of retirement of plant and equipment, the equation illuminates the strategic role of capital formation as the controlling factor and determinant of growth dynamics as, *ceteris paribus*,[31] changes in output are caused by variation of investment and its efficiency. But this is only one interpretation or use to which this equation may be put.

There seem to be sufficient grounds to suppose that correction of some of the flagrant system-made inefficiencies would constitute a significant source of economic growth. But there may not be sufficient grounds to reduce this statement to quantitative terms on tenable assumptions. Even one percentage point rise in u—resulting from a better utilization of, say, underemployed capacity in the machine-building and construction industry—would produce a one percentage point increase in r, not an altogether inconsequential effect.

With m, a, and u constant, the consequence stemming

from the growth equation is that, under the assumed conditions, the share of gross investment in GNP wholly determines the growth pace of GNP. The higher the i, the more rapid will be the growth pace. In the short run consumption would be depressed, but over a sufficiently long extension of the plan horizon the reduction in the share of consumption should be compensated for by the rising Y. The benefit is likely to be greater the more extended the time interval for the duration of the dynamic process that we take into consideration. The long-term benefits are inversely related to the size of m.

With the constancy of parametric framework (m, a, and u), the size of r would vary directly with i. In addition, if constancy of i should be postulated, the size of r would be steady over time. The stability of i means that investment increases at the same rate as Y, that the same rate of growth of investment as that of national income is a vehicle for a steady growth of Y, i.e., the rate of growth of investment does not need to outpace the growth of national product in order to maintain steady growth. *Ceteris paribus,* growth rates could be accelerated only by increasing i, and consequently the share of accumulation in national product must rise faster than Y and, *ipso facto,* consumption, whose share in national product will decline (will grow more slowly than Y). The adoption of a higher growth rate as a desideratum is tantamount, *ceteris paribus,* to the reduction in the share of current consumption. This is one of the constraints imposed on the planners in the choice of (or maximization of) the growth rate.

Kalecki's approach to growth processes stressed the strategic role of determining a realistic i and focused on the ensuing costs of various rates in terms of short-run consumption. While the inter-temporal choice is customarily presented as a resolution of the conflict between present and future consumption, the problem is vastly complicated as the "future" can be interpreted as a time interval of varied lengths. The resolution of conflicts between immediate burdens and more or less distant benefits for the present generation is the crucial choice, where it is not only the overall size of consumption during that period that matters, but where the time distribution is the key issue.

In order to achieve a higher level of consumption in the long run, it is necessary to impose real hardships or restraints on the living standards in the more immediate future. Kalecki stressed the immediate consumption effects of growth policies. He was adamant in his stand on the content of the Polish perspective plan:

> Nearly two years ago I was shown a working paper on setting the share of investment in national income with the aim of maximizing total consumption for the long-range plan period. Through mathematical analysis the method offered not too attractive results: it showed that for a twenty-year period productive investments should constitute about 80 percent of national income. This is not even as bizarre as it might appear; a high share of productive investments in national income allows for its high rate of growth and this so raises its level in the following years of the long-range plan that consumption not only in those years, but even for the entire period of the plan, is higher than with a lower share of investment in national income. But that which is comprehensible is not always reasonable: even if one would not be concerned with the suffering of the unfortunate population in the first years of the long-term plan, one would have to take into account that, with the assumed standard of living, this population would soon perish and thus would be unable to fulfill the plan.[32]

Logically, in Kalecki's approach the emphasis is on the cardinal importance of the investment and foreign trade efficiency analyses, as, *celeris paribus,* changes in the growth rate are traceable to changes in investment rate and/or impact of capital formation in terms of increase (change) of national product. Incessant increases in the investment rate must encounter various barriers and ceilings which will, *inter alia,* prolong the period of gestation and fruition, thus reducing the efficiency of investment.

Kalecki discussed the question of choice of a growth rate by concentrating and identifying key states of labor supply as factors circumscribing the planners' maneuverability. The question is: How should growth be accelerated if labor supply is not a limiting factor? With essentially exhausted labor reserves, growth can be speeded up only by raising productivity. Productivity may be increased by means of changing one (or a combination of) parameter(s) in the growth equation. In proceeding further from a simpler to a more complex analysis, it is necessary to relax the assumed parametric scaffolding and to examine the impact of variability of the hitherto constant parameters.

Under conditions where a reserve of labor prevails, as in an underdeveloped country, the economy may benefit by reducing the investment-output ratio (m), i.e., by applying less capital-intensive and more labor-intensive techniques per unit of output wherever technically feasible. The advantages of such measures consist in (1) raising the growth rate of output without reducing the share of consumption in national product, or (2) raising the level of consumption without decelerating the growth pace of output.

Kalecki emphasized that more capital-intensive production is per se neither superior nor inferior. The choice of a "correct" capital intensity of production depends on the state of the labor supply and the prevailing trend of progress of techniques, with allowance for technical limitations of substitution and an imposition of a "floor" of real wages per unit of labor employed as a constraint.

To observe the principle of efficiency of planned investments means to achieve a given increment of national income, with the aid of the smallest possible investment resources, while ensuring equilibrium of manpower and foreign trade balances. The lower the productive investments indispensable for achieving the assumed increment of national income, the higher will be the part of this increment which could be earmarked for consumption.

Industrialization is not an end in itself but an instrument for maintaining an equilibrium in the balance of manpower and payments, with a given rate of growth of national income; the same is true for the rise of labor productivity. A saving of manpower can be achieved by different means and, *ceteris paribus,* the variant with the lowest investment outlays should be chosen. No purpose is served by saving labor through costly automation if this can be achieved with smaller outlays through the primitive mechanization of "yardwork." The often encountered opinion that the best equipment is always that which is at the highest world technical standard is fallacious: what is best can be determined only by a calculation of investment efficiency and depends on economic circumstances. It is not necessarily true that what is profitable for an American concern must also be profitable in Poland. Effective production depends not only on a saving of labor, but also on a saving of investment resources.

If the capital intensity of new equipment is too low, then, with an assumed rate of growth of national income, there will be shortages of manpower; if it is too high, there will be underutilization of labor resources. In the first case the plan cannot be executed, and in the second it is irrational because it assumes unnecessarily high investment outlays and burdens on current consumption, with a simultaneous underutilization of the labor force.[33] A policy of advocating an increase in the capital-output ratio even under conditions of unlimited labor supply seems to be favored, *inter alia*, by Maurice Dobb and A. K. Sen.[34] Kalecki's analysis ultimately leads him to the conclusion that growth acceleration probably has no major practical significance under conditions of unlimited labor supply. The argument rests mainly on the assumed relative values of increasing the labor productivity owing to technical progress, while Dobb and Sen have not taken this type of growth of productivity into consideration at all. According to them, the assumed values for the increase of productivity are to be achieved solely by raising the capital-output ratio.[35]

Acceleration or stabilization of the growth rate may encounter various barriers. The sources of additional labor are not inexhaustible. With the exhaustion of labor reserves, the dynamics of growth processes are constrained by the rate of growth of productivity, mainly a function of technological progress, and by the natural rate of increase of the labor force. Under such conditions it would be undesirable to raise the rate of investment (i), for it would result merely in an *underutilization* of productive capacity due to a shortage of labor to man the equipment. If, at the postulated growth rate, labor barriers are likely to occur it might be necessary in order to overcome these barriers to increase the share of investment so as to favor mechanization as a substitution for labor (or partly by autarky and forcing ineffective exports to pay for rising imports, requiring in turn an increase of i). With no labor reserves to be tapped, the target increases in the growth rate may be ensured only by accelerating the rise of labor productivity by means of either/or, or combinations of, (1) variation of the capital-output ratio, i.e., increasing m, (2) shortening the life span of capital assets, which leads to an increase in the parameter of amortization (a), and (3) more effective utilization of existing productive capacities as a result of improvements in planning, organization, etc., i.e., measures reflected in the rise of the size of the coefficient of improvement independent of investment activity (u).

The exhaustion of untapped labor reserves imposes constraints on the growth rate under the assumed conditions of the constancy of parametric framework (constant m). There is usually a choice of techniques to produce a given output. Within a certain range, labor and investments (capital) are substitutable inputs. The quantum of investment (labor) per unit of output may vary substantially from one production technique to another, Application of more mechanized production processes saves labor by substituting investment (varied quantities of investment, pending the shape or movement along the isoquant, compensate for a saving of a unit of labor without affecting the quantity of output produced). But substitution of capital (investment) for labor necessarily entails additional investment per unit of national product.[36]

A labor shortage does not inhibit the growth rate but can be overcome by the substitution effect, entailing additional investments per unit of national product; that is, necessitating a rise in i to achieve the target growth rate r. It is quite possible that innovation may consist merely in substitution of labor by machine (labor saving) without affecting the volume of output produced. In such a case m would necessarily rise. While this is plausible, it is by no means necessarily the prevailing type of progress in techniques. (For instance, in the case of automation machines not only replace workers but also speed up production processes.)

Kalecki is noncommittal about the kind of prevailing technical progress, concentrating on analyzing the consequences of three key types: encouraging capital usage, discouraging capital usage, and neutral. He defines technical progress as being of the neutral variety when an increase in the investment-output ratio results in a one-shot increase in labor productivity in newly commissioned plants, but does not enhance the pace of growth of productivity. In the case of the neutral type of technical progress, the growth tempo of labor productivity is independent of the size of *m* (the productivity of labor in new plants increases at a constant rate).

Technical progress is defined as "encouraging capital usage" if an increase of *m* causes a once-and-for-all increase in labor productivity, while the tempo of growth of productivity increases with *m* (the rate of increase of productivity is greater the larger the size of *m*). Technical progress is termed as "discouraging capital usage" when a rise in *m*, while bringing about a rise in the level of productivity in new plants, leads simultaneously to a decline in the rate of increase of labor productivity.[37]

The prevailing variety of technical progress does not prejudge the path of economic development to be followed. The fact that technical progress is of the type "encouraging capital intensity" does not necessarily mean that the investment-output ratio is bound to rise. Even if *m* is maintained on the same level, some regular increase in the growth rate of productivity will be obtained in newly commissioned capacities. By contrast, in the case of technical progress of the neutral variety, *m* does not necessarily have to be unaltered. Through gradual shifting to higher *m*, it is possible to accelerate the growth tempo of productivity by moving along (to the right, i.e., substituting investment for labor) the isoquant as it shifts toward origin under the impact of forces of technical progress. Such a policy maneuver to speed up the growth pace of productivity (output) by "superimposing substitution" (extra growth over and above that owed to technical progress) is much more attractive when progress is of the "encouraging capital usage" variety since then the gain in dynamics of productivity is reinforced by the advantages of a higher growth tempo of productivity associated with higher investment-output ratios.

Kalecki assailed the dogmatic proposition that technical advancement always leads to a rising organic composition of capital (higher capital intensity) and necessarily entails faster growth of the capital goods-producing sector. It is primarily the type of technical progress that is decisive for the relative growth rate of capital formation and national product (relative growth pace of producers' and consumers' goods sectors). For example, growth of investment at the same rate as that of national product ensures a steady growth pace of national product. Expanded reproduction (growth) at a steady rate does not necessarily require a faster rate of growth of capital formation than that of national product.

Among the factors imposing limits on the choice of growth rate, the difficulties of equilibrating the balance of payments stand out as one of the most growth-inhibiting barriers. The foreign trade barrier is higher the higher the target growth rate. Indeed, the obstacle to a very high rate of growth

> is the very high capital outlay required both directly and as a result of difficulties in equilibrating the balance of foreign trade and possibly also of the shortage of labor; in fact, *the difficulties in foreign trade may make it virtually impossible to exceed a certain level of the growth rate.*[38]

During the course of economic development the demand for imports is accelerated. In the absence of credit financing exports are required to pay for the growing imports. The higher the growth rate, the more rapidly must exports rise and the greater the difficulties encountered in selling in foreign markets (especially finished products like machinery) in view of the limited foreign demand for the exportables of a given country. *Ceteris paribus,* a higher growth rate will require a greater production of exportables and a greater marketing effort, or it will require that some imports be replaced by domestic production.[39] Depending on demand elasticities, efforts to sell a larger physical volume will probably be accompanied by a deterioration of the terms of trade, accompanied by a price reduction for certain goods on certain markets, a change in the structure of exports requiring higher inputs, shifts to less profitable markets, and a continuous forcing of products whose exchange becomes increasingly less effective (or more ineffective) so as to pay for the rapid growth of import requirements. Since rapid growth of export revenue is unlikely, the gap between import requirements and imports widens. The pressures accumulate and the foreign trade barrier becomes insurmountable. Usually uncontrolled deceleration sets in first, followed by a throttling down of growth by the system's directors. Moreover, as the growth rate of national income (industrial output) flags, import requirements decrease at a faster rate, the pressures on the balance of payments are eased, and the foreign trade barrier is lowered.

When national product grows at a precipitously high rate, the expansion of some sectors (branches) lags behind needs because of certain technological and organizational "ceilings." The planners work under constraints (they must recognize long-term growth bottlenecks). An increase in investments is not always a "solution," for it might not be helpful in increasing the rate of output expansion beyond a certain point. The factors that limit the rate of expansion of individual branches (sectors) and that hamper the overall pace of growth of production are varied, and include:

1. Limited natural resources.

2. Bottlenecks of sufficiently qualified personnel. An abrupt rise in investment activity contributes to the scattering of unfinished construction and to the extension of the protracted time of construction, thus reducing efficiency of investment. With a given rate of capital formation in a particular industry, the number of projects under construction is in proportion to the construction period. If the period is protracted and the investment activity stupendous, the number of projects is so large that the existing technical and managerial personnel are incapable of effectively handling the manifold and expanding projects. In such a situation the most potent medicine is generally to reduce the volume of investment activity. If, in spite of the situation, the high rate of investment activity is maintained (or increased), the results are counterproductive. Obviously, the longevity of the period of gestation is further extended, resulting in freezing more capital instead of expanding the output of the given industry.

3. Difficulties in recruiting workers for particular occupations (especially acute problems in staffing coal mines).

4. Large amounts of time spent in mastering new techniques and learning by doing.

5. Difficulties in adopting technical improvements. Agricultural production is a special case. The greatest difficulties of introducing new production processes are usually encountered in agriculture where there always persist some elements of spontaneity in the development of production.

Foreign trade difficulties may create an almost insurmountable barrier, preventing the rate of expansion from exceeding a certain level. In fact, at a certain growth rate attempts to balance imports with exports do not produce effective results. Further reduction of export prices is pointless if the result of increased physical volume produces no increments to revenue as the additional revenue from an additional quantity sold is smaller than the loss resulting from the reduction of prices on goods previously sold (within a certain range, demand is inelastic).

As a rule, drives to maintain a higher growth rate than the economy can sustain under prevailing conditions will produce a reduction of the efficiency of investments and foreign trade and general conditions of overheating of the economy, with widespread repercussions resulting in the decline of the efficiency of the entire production process. The growing gaps have to be made up for by foreign trade (production of substitutes or withdrawal of resources from the consumption fund). Efforts to increase exports or anti-import measures are likely to result in higher costs in terms of investment and labor inputs. A given volume of investments (quantum of resources) will thus produce a smaller increment of national product (a given i will yield a lower r). With difficulties in balancing foreign trade, a smaller relative rise in growth rate corresponds to a given increase in the relative rate of investment, as if no such difficulties were encountered.

The dilemma of allocation of resources between consumption in the present (short run) and accumulation for the future and the various growth barriers, long-term bottlenecks, and ceilings appearing under the guise of difficulties in equilibrating foreign trade, constitute the core of the real growth problems of a socialist economy.

In development plans the estimate of the impact of foreign trade on the rise of national product is always very hypothetical in character. This uncertainty as to the planned magnitudes of the foreign trade variable should lead to the adoption of a rather conservative estimate and, ultimately, to the choice of a relatively lower target growth rate. To the extent that long-term agreements between socialist countries eliminate such uncertainty, a relatively higher r may be favored. By predetermining the bulk of the future foreign trade of the socialist countries, long-term trade agreements between them contribute to the acceleration of their rate of expansion. However, such trade agreements do not solve, *inter alia,* the difficulties of marketing increased exports. If the other party is unwilling to accept an increased volume of certain products, it is necessary to ship less profitable products or to pre-empt products indispensable for domestic expansion, and sometimes it may even be impossible to raise exports beyond a certain level.

While the various ceilings and barriers limiting the rate of growth would generally be less acute in a self-sufficient economy, they are not likely to disappear. But with high rates of growth, the rate of expansion of output of particular industries will trail behind the rising requirements due to the impact of technological and organizational factors. The factors inhibiting economic expansion would be further accentuated in the absence of indirect production. There would be no possibility of filling the widening gaps—that is, of reducing or alleviating domestic shortages and tensions—by securing the required commodities through imports. The imports could be procured in exchange for those commodities whose rate of expansion can be increased without encountering (within a relevant range) technological barriers, that is, demand-determined industries. (On the other hand, the rate of growth of output in the case of supply-determined industries is restricted, where, due to the technical and organizational barriers, flow of output cannot be accelerated even by considerably increasing investments in them.) In the case of development policy favoring autarky, the only possible approach to overcoming or alleviating enduring bottlenecks would be to produce domestic substitutes for the products persistently in short supply, so in many cases it is likely to be more costly than if imports were secured by producing exports.

V

The Polish 1961–1975 perspective plan,[40] prepared by Kalecki and his staff at the Perspective Plan Institute of the Planning Commission and the Central Commission on the Perspective Plan, is so far unquestionably still the most consistent, complete, and scrupulously elaborated perspective plan in the history of economic planning in Eastern Europe (including the USSR). Furthermore, as the practical embodiment of the application of Kalecki's theory of growth under socialism, it differs diametrically from the voluntaristic approach which characterizes traditional Soviet-type planning (at least since the advent of the first Five-Year Plan in the USSR).

The initial step in drafting a perspective plan is to roughly outline the plan, assuming a high rate of growth in comparison to past experience which, if necessary, can be reduced at the initial testing stage. The next step is to assume a capital coefficient, again on the basis of past experience (or the experience of other countries), taking into account as much as possible the specificities of the period and the economic circumstances of the country in question. At any rate, this will only be a rough approximation, for the capital coefficient largely depends on the structure of the increase of output, which may vary greatly from that of past experience or of other countries.

With a given coefficient, the first approximation to the annual productive investment in the perspective plan can be arrived at. The problem of the coefficient's relating to the increment in inventories is similarly handled. The total of consumption and unproductive investment at the beginning, end, and middle of the perspective plan can be arrived at by subtracting productive investment and the increase of inventories from national income. Although it will still be largely arbitrary, some sort of decision for splitting the total consumption and unproductive investments into its two components can be arrived at by comparing the resulting level of consumption of consumer goods with the capacity constraint of fixed assets yielding consumer services (e.g., the per capita dwelling space).

It may already be found at this stage that the relative share of productive investment, plus the increase in inventories in national income, is too high because it impinges on short-run consumption and unproductive investments. But even so the variant could be entertained somewhat further because of the hypothetical nature of the capital coefficient on which the result largely depends.

At the next stage, a broad outline of the industrial structure is attempted. Having allocated national income to its four major components, a reasonable assumption as to the future structure of consumption has to be made, taking as a pattern that of the more developed countries, with particular attention to the local conditions or income elasticities of demand derived from family budgets. Then the industrial structure can be roughly outlined. This information is required for testing the balance of trade and for achieving a second approximation of the capital coefficient that would mirror the structure of the increase in output.

At this juncture two types of industries (including all branches of economic activity, such as agriculture, transportation, etc.) should be distinguished: supply-determined and demand-determined industries. The former embrace the activities whose long-range growth rates are restricted by certain technical and organizational ceilings, as previously outlined, so that the rate of their output cannot be accelerated even by pouring considerably more investment into them. At least for the range of growth rates of national income considered, no such ceilings exist for the demand-determined industries. Consequently, demand for the output of these industries can condition its increase in the long run.

When the volume of productive and unproductive investment, the increase in inventories, and the volume and structure of consumption are known, domestic demand for products of various branches of the economy can be roughly estimated. This requires some assumption of input-output coefficients, with allowance for postulated technical advancement trends. In the case of a supply-determined industry, it can be determined whether any output remains for export or whether import is necessary to supplement domestic production. The list of import requirements would also include those goods which cannot be domestically produced. Allowances would have to be made for domestically produced substitutes for imported goods.

The first approximation of the total demand for imports will thus be arrived at. The value of exports provided by the surplus output of supply-determined industries will be subtracted from the value of total import requirements to obtain the value of exports which still have to be provided by the output of demand-determined industries. Output of the demand-determined industries will be set so as to cover domestic requirements for their products and the balance of the above-mentioned export requirements.

The question then arises whether a problem in the balance of trade really comes up, since imports must automatically be covered by exports. However, the balance of foreign trade so arrived at may be of no substance in practice, where problems may arise in foreign sales preventing the fulfillment of envisaged export plans. The terms of trade may so deteriorate that the inflow of foreign exchange may not be sufficient to cover purchases abroad. Furthermore, even if this purpose can be achieved very high capital expenditures may be required in comparison to the effect in terms of foreign exchange, which may further exacerbate the problem of the relative share of investment in national income.

The export plan must be scrutinized from the standpoint of *practical execution*. The rate of growth would have to be scaled down if this program should prove to be tenuous. The restoration of the balance of foreign trade would be much helped by this action, together with the unchanged expansion of supply-determined industries. This action will cause a considerable drop in the demand for imports and possibly a substantial increase in the surplus of output of the supply-determined industries available for export.

Even if the foreign trade targets appear to be fairly down-to-earth, the expansion of exports may bring such pressure to bear on capital expenditures that the variant in question may have to be foregone because of inroads into short-run consumption.

Before estimating the necessary investments, a "balance"

of requirements and availability for labor has to be drawn, with allowances for increase in productivity stemming from technical progress. If a labor shortage is imminent, more outlays have to be provided for mechanization and modernization which, again, will inflate investment expenditures.

A more specific estimate of total productive investments can now be made. It may diverge considerably from that arrived at on the basis of the hypothetical capital coefficient. It could happen at this juncture that even though it is possible to arrive at a balance of foreign trade on the basis of the assumed growth rate, the estimated relative share of productive investment in national income may prove to be unacceptable. Again, the rate of growth would have to be scaled down and the new variant examined as outlined above.

The adopted variant should feature the highest possible rate of growth at which there is a realistic possibility of equilibrating foreign trade and at which the relative share of productive investment plus the increase in inventories in national income is considered tolerable by the authorities from the standpoint of the impact on consumption and unproductive investment in the short run.

It is evident that the perspective plan was not built along the lines of the traditional method of plan construction that starts out by assuming the more or less arbitrary target rates of expansion of individual branches of the economy. In a plan constructed along traditional lines, shortages in some branches and surpluses in others can be expected. There is a tendency to maintain the high indexes of "surplus" branches, especially when they pertain to branches whose rapid development is taken to symbolize, and is identified with, economic and technical progress (e.g., electric power and machine building). This is a fallacious approach for it leads to a swelling of planned requirements for the products involved, or to the classification of a surplus of a given product as reserve. Obviously, plan reserves are particularly useful, but they should be formed in endangered areas ("susceptible activities") and not arbitrarily, with the aim of maintaining a high index equated with progress. In practice, such surplus indexes are wasteful, either because requirements are swollen already at the planning stage or because unnecessary reserves are created which whet the appetite and can be instrumental in increasing requirements during plan execution.

In spite of formal ("on paper") balancing, when optimistic or so-called mobilizing plan indexes are assumed their execution becomes at best unsure (particularly in view of material shortages and disturbances in foreign trade). Optimism can appear in different areas: in setting the material usage norms, in forecasting the use of the existing production apparatus and the construction and trial-run periods of new projects and modernization, in evaluating export possibilities, and finally in estimating investment costs. In the latter case, the optimism of the planner is compounded by the fact that enterprises urge the undertaking of a given investment by presenting it in the best possible light, so that after it has been included in the plan the cost estimate could be radically revised.

The "mobilizing effect" of optimistic indexes, if it is not based on concrete measures, such as raw materials-saving investments, is particularly questionable. They mobilize mainly toward ingenious product-mix manipulations, a more or less apparent deterioration of quality, etc. This is the rise of the phenomenon of a taut plan—an ambitious plan, but risky and not fully realistic. If such a plan misfires, as it often does, it usually involves losses and costs of change, i.e., the result is worse than that which could have been achieved with more cautious planning. A realistic plan is so set that the risk of its unfulfillment should be minimized.

VI

People can be admired for many things. Nature endowed Michal Kalecki with a brilliant and fascinating mind, a clarity of thought, the precious ability to grasp the essentials of a problem, a lucid perception of interdependencies, and the great gift of seeing the forest when most of us only perceive the trees. One of the greatest delights was to observe his mind in action. Then his frail and almost fragile body transformed itself into a gigantic and imposing presence. He often electrified his interlocutors and commanded boundless respect (even from people of opposite opinions) for the iron-clad logic of his arguments. He was laconic, austere, and concise in his presentation, which might have contributed to the fact that his works are not as widely read and understood as they deserve to be. He often became impatient when asked to elaborate on a point. His incisive mind did not readily grasp that others' thinking processes were inferior to his. Perhaps his apparent impatience also sprang from his ability to identify the relevant or quantitatively important set of variables, and his conviction that the crucial problems were the ones to concentrate on. He often became quite irritated if one attempted to shift the discussion to what he considered secondary issues.

Although Kalecki had a good working knowledge of mathematics, he considered that economists who are interested in mathematical niceties, rather than in the economic problems, have missed their vocation as mathematicians.

He felt that there were far too many urgent economic problems affecting the welfare of society awaiting solution to concentrate on refinements of not immediately relevant theories: "Theories are being created which may raise problems of great interest but are not very conducive to understanding what actually happened, is happening or should be happening." [41]

For example, he stressed that growth models are often built on the assumption of *laissez-faire* and do not assign the crucial and empirically relevant role to the government sector, to the state's widespread intervention, and to the interaction between the state and private sectors. The institutional framework of a social system exerts a strong impact on its economic dynamics. A theory of growth must be relevant to that system. Attempts in Western economics to construct a general theory of growth by building models quite remote from the realities of modern capitalist, socialist, or developing economies do not grasp the realities of different social systems. Most of the literature relates, at least by implication, to some sort of idealized model of *laissez-faire* capitalism.

> There *is* probably some interconnection between government intervention and these models [of *laissez-faire* capitalism] but rather psychological in character: the high level of employment creates a climate favorable to their construction being unperturbed by the problem of effective demand.[42]

Kalecki saw no relevance in some economists' preoccupation with allocating resources to alternative uses when those resources are underemployed. He considered that resources are misallocated in those socialist economies that invest most of their energies in improving their models of functioning when actually the crucial issue is the share, pattern, and efficiency of investment in national income.

During the Polish discussion on the economic model (1956–1958), Kalecki questioned whether under Polish conditions it would be feasible to introduce a price system leading to an effective allocation of resources and replacing central distribution of materials. The producers' flexibility and speed of adjustment is likely not to be sufficient to overcome bottlenecks. He contended that substantial and frequent price changes might be necessary to induce the desired effect on the suppliers' part, and felt that such a method would not be very practical under such conditions of strenuous tensions. Under such conditions the system of central allocation is simpler, more expedient, and more effective. Correctives through varying the production flows by the central planner are likely to be more certain measures.[43]

His unpopular statements about the limited results that can be expected from improvements in the model of functioning of the socialist economy logically follow from his analysis of the growth propellers and barriers. Kalecki also maintained that the introduction of elaborate incentive schemes requires a vast bureaucratic network to differentiate skills, to take into account different levels of technical equipment, etc. In order for the schemes to work they would have to be differentiated so as to relate the productivity of a sub-unit, and this would also require cumbersome and costly bureaucratic machinery.

VII

Michal Kalecki commanded the highest respect and admiration not only for the analytical powers and clarity of his thought, but for his very high personal integrity and principles. His attitude at the time of publication of Keynes's *General Theory* is an example of scholarly behavior *par excellence.* His career can be described as a chain of resignations that were acts of conscience (tinged with stubbornness), often protests against prejudice, discrimination, and tyranny. He was deeply disturbed by human suffering and poverty and was fervently dedicated to the ideals of socialism, which he believed to be the most conducive system for solving these problems.

Kalecki was a man of inordinate modesty. He once remarked that men could be classified upward according to the time they spent thinking about themselves and other members of the human race. He would have been at the very top of the list. He was a man of great courage, warm heart, compassion, and understanding kindness. He possessed a wonderful sense of humor which he sometimes used to ridicule adversaries. Few people could remain indifferent to him. He was either loved or thoroughly disliked. Kalecki never hesitated to express his views sharply and boldly, albeit not very diplomatically. While in personal dealings he was always extremely careful not to offend, in matters of economics he was merciless and would never surrender. He cared only about the logic of the argument, thereby antagonizing those who did not know him well and were offended by his polemics.

Kalecki did not care for any official recognition, positions, or titles, nor did he seek popularity. He never "promoted" his ideas. He was a man of extreme personal honesty, the highest standards of moral behavior (which even his most devoted admirers find difficult to emulate), very hard working, and overly scrupulous and exacting in performing assumed responsibilities. He would forgive almost any imperfection in human beings, but could not forgive a lack of integrity or unethical behavior. His difficult life was comforted by having found a true friend and companion in his wife. Ada Kalecki was totally and unselfishly devoted to him.

Kalecki's formal university education was in engineering at the Warsaw Polytechnic and then at the Gdansk Polytechnic, which, due to financial difficulties, he had to leave in 1923 just before graduating.[44] However, his interest in economics was born during his academic training. Until 1929, when he became associated with the Institute of Research on Business Cycles and Prices, then under the directorship of Professor Edward Lipinski, Kalecki held temporary jobs in Lodz and Warsaw and was engaged in research on business cycles and on the structure of large firms. At the Institute he cooperated with Ludvik Landau and was involved, *inter alia,* in research on the Polish national income. In 1933 he published his book *Próba teorii koniunktury (An Essay in the Theory of Business Cycle),* which is a summary of his research for a number of years and lays down in broad lines the foundations of what has become known as the "Keynesian revolution" in economics.

In 1936, with the support of the Rockefeller Foundation, he went to Sweden and then to England. We have already described the events that surrounded the meeting and interaction with Keynes and the Keynesians. While in England, Kalecki learned of the dismissal of his two close colleagues at the Institute of Research on Business Cycles and Prices and resigned in protest. Early in 1940 he obtained a post at the Oxford Institute of Statistics. He became involved in statistical and economic analysis of various aspects of the war economy in Britain. At the Oxford Institute he cooperated with many outstanding British and international economists and vastly contributed to the outstanding achievements of the Institute, of which he was the moving spirit. Among his contributions during that period one should note particularly the study of rationing. The scheme he evolved was very similar to that later adopted when rationing was introduced. But perhaps his most outstanding contributions of the war period were to the economics of full employment and to the elaboration of the theory of economic dynamics.

From 1946 to 1955 Kalecki served as Deputy Director of the Department of Economic Affairs of the United Nations Secretariat in charge of preparing the World Economic Reports. He resigned that post as a result of McCarthyist pressures. On his return to Poland he became economic advisor to the Office of the Council of Ministers and later (1957–1960) to the Planning Commission, where he headed the Commission for Perspective Planning. The celebrated, controversial, and never adopted perspective plan for the Polish economy was prepared under his guidance. He was also Deputy Chairman of the Economic Council until its demise in 1963. Until recently he was the Chairman of the Polish delegation to the Economic Commission of COMECON. Concurrently he pursued an active research and academic career. In 1956 (at the age of 57) he received the title of Professor—his first academic title. In 1957 he was elected corresponding member of the Polish Academy of Sciences, and in 1966 he became a full member. In 1964 Warsaw and Wroclaw universities bestowed on him doctor *honoris causa* degrees. He was awarded many state prizes and distinctions. In 1961 he took a teaching post at the Central School of Planning and Statistics where he taught the theory of business cycles and growth of capitalist and socialist economies. During that period he became increasingly concerned with the problems of developing economies. He helped create and nurtured during its formative years the Department of Economic Problems in Developing Countries created by Warsaw University and by the Central School of Planning and Statistics.

In 1968 Kalecki retired voluntarily in protest against the dismissal of many colleagues who fell victim to the wave of repression against alleged "revisionists" and "Zionists." The last years of his life were filled with many grave disappointments.

During Easter Term 1969 Kalecki was an Overseas Fellow of Churchill College and Faculty Visitor to the Faculty of Economics and Politics at Cambridge University, surrounded by his great admirers. His University Lecture on the theories of growth under various social systems was a great event. Cambridge students, brought up on his writings, packed the hall to its utmost capacity (with many of them crouching on the floor and steps) and gave him a resounding ovation when he entered. It is characteristic of Kalecki's appeal as a lecturer and of the soundness of his logic and arguments that his audience was even more enthusiastic when he finished.

Kalecki's work has earned an enduring place in the history of economic analysis and brought honor to Poland in the realm of achievements in economic science. His work is our legacy and it will continue to inspire new generations of economists. He exerted himself to the very last to enrich this world to which he gave so much and from which he asked and got so little. Economic science has not only lost one of its guiding lights, but humanity is bereft of one of its most ardent champions.

Notes

1. Joan Robinson, Introduction to Michal Kalecki, *Studies in the Theory of Business Cycles, 1933–1939* (Oxford: Basil Blackwell, 1966), pp. viii–ix.
2. Cf. *inter alia* Lawrence R. Klein, *The Keynesian Revolution,* 2nd ed. (New York: Macmillan Co., 1966); Joan Robinson, "Kalecki and Keynes," in *Problems of Economic Dynamics and Planning: Essays in Honour of Michal Kalecki* (London: Perga-

mon Press, 1966); and George L. Shackle, *The Years of High Theory: Invention and Tradition in Economic Thought, 1926–1939* (New York: Cambridge University Press, 1967).

3. "Keynes could never make head or tail of Marx."—Joan Robinson, "Kalecki and Keynes," p. 338. See also Joan Robinson, *Collected Economic Papers, I* (Oxford: Basil Blackwell, 1951), pp. 133–45.
4. Kalecki, *Studies in the Theory of Business Cycles,* p. 1.
5. Lawrence R. Klein, "The Life of John Maynard Keynes," *Journal of Political Economy* (October 1951), pp. 447–48.
6. See Robinson, "Kalecki and Keynes," p. 337.
7. G. L. S. Shackle told me recently that when he met Kalecki at the London School of Economics, what Professor Shackle considers a "non-equivalent exchange" took place: Shackle undertook to help Kalecki perfect his English while Kalecki explained "Keynesian economics" to Shackle.
8. Robinson, "Kalecki and Keynes," p. 339.
9. Ibid., p. 337.
10. The original essay was published in Polish in 1933 as "An Essay on the Theory of Business Cycle," and was subsequently included in *Studies in the Theory of Business Cycles* as "Outline of a Theory of the Business Cycle."
11. Robinson, Introduction to *Studies in the Theory of Business Cycles,* p. xii.
12. Klein, "The Life of John Maynard Keynes," p. 448.
13. "We must record Keynes's acknowledgments of indebtedness [in the construction of the *General Theory*], which in all cases can be independently established, to Mrs. Joan Robinson, Mr. R. G. Hawtrey, Mr. R. F. Harrod, but especially to Mr. R. F. Kahn, whose share in the historic achievement cannot have fallen very far short of co-authorship."—Joseph A. Schumpeter, *History of Economic Analysis* (New York: Oxford University Press, 1954), p. 1172.
14. Robinson, "Kalecki and Keynes," p. 337.
15. On the divergencies between Kalecki's and Keynes's models, see ibid., pp. 337–38.
16. Michal Kalecki, *Theory of Economic Dynamics: An Essay on Cyclical and Long-Run Changes in Capitalist Economy* (New York: Monthly Review Press, 1965).
17. See Robinson, Introduction to *Studies in the Theory of Business*

Cycles, p. xi; and Paulo Sylos-Labini, *Oligopoly and Technical Progress* (Cambridge: Harvard University Press, 1962, 1969).

18. Kalecki, *Studies in the Theory of Business Cycles,* p. 1.
19. Robinson, *Collected Economic Papers, II,* p. 241. On the degree of monopoly and Kalecki's theorem of the distribution of national income, see Sylos-Labini, *Oligopoly and Technical Progress,* pp. 96–100 and passim.
20. Roy Harrod, "Optimum Investment for Growth," in *Problems of Economic Dynamics and Planning,* p. 179. Cf. *The Collected Scientific Papers of Paul Samuelson* (Cambridge: MIT Press, 1966), Vol. I, p. 591, and Vol. II, p. 1695.
21. L. R. Klein, "The Role of Econometrics in Socialist Economics," in *Problems of Economic Dynamics and Planning,* p. 189.
22. Ibid., p. 191. See also Kalecki's novel treatment of the reconciliation of "Econometric Model and Historical Materialism," in *On Political Economy and Econometrics: Essays in Honour of Oskar Lange* (London: Pergamon Press, 1965), pp. 233–38.
23. "Piero Sraffa teased me, saying that I treated Marx as a little-known forerunner of Kalecki. There is a certain sense in which this is not a joke. There are many pointers in *Capital* to a theory of effective demand."—Joan Robinson, Preface to *An Essay on Marxian Economics,* 2nd ed. (New York: St. Martin, 1967), p. vi.
24. Michal Kalecki, "The Problem of Effective Demand with Tugan-Baranowsky and Rosa Luxemburg," in *Selected Essays in the Dynamic of the Capitalist Economy* (Cambridge: Cambridge University Press, 1971), pp. 146–150.
25. Ibid.
26. See Kalecki, *Theory of Economic Dynamics,* pp. 145–61. He related the problems of the determination of investment decisions to the process of economic growth (long-run trend): "The long-run trend is but a slowly changing component of a chain of short-period situations; it has no independent entity." The basic approach applied in the business cycles theory—namely, "establishing two basic relations: one based on the impact of the effective demand generated by investment upon profits and the national income; and the other showing the determination of investment decisions by, broadly speaking, the level and the rate of change of economic activity"—should not be abandoned in confrontation with the problems of long-run growth. The two

basic relations applied in the theory of business cycles "should be formulated in such a way as to yield the trend cum business-cycle phenomenon." Michal Kalecki, "Trend and Business Cycles Reconsidered," *Economic Journal* (June 1968), p. 263.

27. Michal Kalecki, "The Developed and Underdeveloped Capitalist Economy" (in Polish), *Ekonomista,* no. 5 (1966), p. 974.

28. See John Maynard Keynes, *The General Theory of Employment, Interest, and Money* (New York: Harcourt, Brace and World, 1957), p. 245. In her 1949 review of R. F. Harrod's *Towards a Dynamic Economics,* Joan Robinson wrote: "No one will disagree with Mr. Harrod that modern economic theory lacks, and badly needs, a system of analysis dealing with a dynamic society. Keynes' *General Theory of Employment* broke through the husk of static analysis, but, apart from some *obiter dicta,* scarcely developed any theory of long-run development. Mr. Kalecki's pioneering work has been very little followed up . . . many others have shot at a venture into the mists, but we have no systematic body of long-run dynamic theory to supplement this short-period analysis of the General Theory and to swallow up, as a special case, the long-run static theory in which the present generation of academic economists was educated." Joan Robinson, "Mr. Harrod's Dynamics," in *Collected Economic Papers, I,* p. 155. See also *The Theory of Economic Dynamics*; and Evsey D. Domar, *Essays on the Theory of Economic Growth* (New York: Oxford University Press, 1957).

29. Kalecki, "The Problem of Effective Demand with Tugan-Baranowsky and Rosa Luxemburg," pp. 146–150.

30. For the impact of Kalecki's seminal work on changing the mode of analysis of growth processes in long-term planning in Poland (socialist planning), see the following works in Polish: J. Pajestka, *Employment, Investment, and Economic Growth* (Warsaw: 1961), p. 30 and passim; W. Lissowski, "The Question of Determination of the Correct Levels and Directions of Productive Investments in the Perspective Plan," *Gospodarka Planowa,* no. 2 (1958), pp. 9–12; M. Rakowski, "About the Growth Rate in the Perspective Plan," *Gospodarka Planowa,* no. 8 (1956), p. 29; W. Brus and K. Laski, "Problems of the Growth Theory in Socialism," *Ekonomista,* no. 6 (1962), pp. 1293 ff.; K. Laski, *An Outline of the Theory of Reproduction* (Warsaw: 1965). See also J. Sol-

daczuk, Preface to *nternational Trade and Development* (Warsaw: 1966), p. 10, in English.

31. *Inter alia,* given full utilization of existing capacities, similarly to the case of the acceleration principle. See Kalecki, *Theory of Economic Dynamics,* pp. 100–01, 106.
32. Michal Kalecki, "Accumulation and Maximization of Consumption" (in Polish), *Ekonomista,* no. 3 (1962), p. 706.
33. See Michal Kalecki, "On the Fundamental Principles of Long-Term Planning" (in Polish), *Zycie Gospodarcze,* no. 24 (1963).
34. Maurice Dobb, *An Essay on Economic Growth and Planning,* 2nd ed. (New York: Monthly Review Press, 1969), and Amartya K. Sen, *Choice of Techniques: An Aspect of the Theory of Planned Economic Development,* 3rd ed. (New York: Augustus Kelley, 1962). Cf. H. Leibenstein and W. Galenson, "Investment Criteria, Productivity, and Economic Development," *Quarterly Journal of Economics,* August 1955.
35. See Michal Kalecki, *Introduction to the Theory of Growth in a Socialist Economy* (Oxford: Basil Blackwell, 1969), Chapter 10.
36. If an isoquant depicts a unit increment in the national product (of unchanged composition) *i,* the investment outlays plotted on the abscissa simply designate the quantity of investment required to produce a given increment of national product—the investment outlay is equal to the investment-output ratio *m*; that is, the investment outlay per unit increment in national product. The ordinate denotes the labor outlay per unit increment of national product.
37. For a discussion of technical progress repercussions of various types of classifications, see Kalecki, *Introduction to the Theory of Growth,* Chapter 7.
38. Michal Kalecki, *On Economic and Social Questions of People's Poland* (in Polish) (Warsaw, 1964), p. 51. Emphasis added.
39. For example, recent preliminary analysis of the dependence of changes in imports of materials on alterations in the rate of growth of industrial output in Czechoslovakia disclosed that the swings of fluctuations of imports are considerably greater than those of the fluctuation of growth rates of industrial output since a 1 percent increase of output requires, on the average, about a 6 percent increase in imports.
40. Michal Kalecki, "The 1961–1975 Perspective Plan" (in Polish),

Nowe Drogi, no. 8 (1958), pp. 27–54; and *On Economic and Social Questions of People's Poland.*

41. Michal Kalecki, "Theories of Growth in Different Social Systems," *Scientia,* no. 5–6 (1970), p. 311.
42. Ibid., p. 313.
43. Michal Kalecki, *Discussion About the Polish Economic Model* (in Polish) (Warsaw: 1957), pp. 35–36.
44. For a more detailed biographical sketch, see Tadeusz Kowalik, "Biography of Michal Kalecki," in *Problems of Economic Dynamics and Planning,* pp. 1–12, and George R. Feiwel, *The Intellectual Capital of Michal Kalecki* (Knoxville: The University of Tennessee Press), forthcoming.

The Last Phase in the Transformation of Capitalism

Preface
by Włodzimierz Brus

The Last Phase of the Transformation of Capitalism is a rather unusual book: it consists of six short papers of which the first, "Stimulating the Business Upswing in Nazi Germany," was published in the weekly *Polska Gospodarcza* in 1935 and the last, "Vietnam and U.S. Big Business," in the weekly *Polityka* in January 1967. This is a stretch of time covering about one-third of our dramatic century.

There arises an immediate question: Is there any link between these brief essays written over such a long period which justifies their publication at present (with some cuts rather than with additions)? This is for the reader to judge, but the author of this preface does not entertain any doubts on this score. For all these essays exhibit the same idea, important for the understanding of the world of today: in the last decades the knowledge of economic processes and of techniques of government policy in capitalist countries has developed to the point where it is possible to reach and maintain a high degree of employment of capital equipment and labor. In practice, however, taking advantage of these possibilities encounters obstacles rooted in the social and economic structure of capitalism which involve the dominant position of the monopolistic owners of the basic economic resources. This is reflected in the apparently paradoxical phenomenon of resistance against full employment policies except where the situation involves dangerous social tensions. And the resistance will stop altogether where government economic intervention is based on armament expenditures associated with an imperialist expansion abroad and a consolidation of reactionary forces at home.

This leading idea, argued in a condensed but forcible manner, constitutes a warning against dogmatic disregard for the real changes which contemporary capitalism has undergone. The crises of the 1929–1933 variety are no longer imminent. The generally prosperous economic situation, lasting over a long period with intermittent mild and short depressions, could not fail to have an important impact on the social and political position of the working class in developed capitalist countries, especially in the United States. It is true, of course, that the standard of living of the broad masses is much below what it could be because of the waste usually involved in government intervention as actually practiced; but the standard is also much higher than that which would be associated with the underutilization of resources occurring in a *laissez-faire* economy.

Kalecki also denies in his analysis of underdeveloped countries the frequently assumed inability of the middle classes to play the role of a ruling class (see the last paper in this book on "Intermediate Regimes," originally published in *Polityka* in October 1966 but for reasons of logic put at the end of this collection). The "intermediate regimes" of a number of underdeveloped countries, controlled by a *sui generis* amalgamation of the middle classes with state capitalism, may under present historical conditions become a lasting phenomenon and must not be considered either as purely capitalist or as naturally evolving toward socialism.

But these essays contain yet another warning no less important and somewhat more general in character: a warning against the fascination of technical aspects of economics, leading to the treatment of economic processes as socially neutral phenomena. It is no accident that in each paper, implicitly or explicitly—and especially in "Political Aspects of Full Employment," published in England in 1943 in the *Political Quarterly*—the analysis of complex economic phenomena is closely interconnected with that of political problems. "Vietnam and U.S. Big Business" is also very significant from this point of view: the aim and prospects of American aggression in Vietnam are considered jointly with the directions and methods of government economic policy and the interrelation between this policy and the interests of different big business groups.

Economics presented in this little volume is *political* economy worthy of the name: a discipline which shows us the social relations, in particular the class and group conflicts, behind the economic quantitative relations. For the form and the consequences of government intervention in the capitalist economy can be grasped only if an analysis of the economic mechanisms is accompanied by an analysis of the social forces which propel these mechanisms.

The application of Marxian methodology in the broad sense yields results of great interest *inter alia* because, as mentioned, the essays cover a long stretch of time. The fact that the collection starts with "Stimulating the Business Upswing in Nazi Germany" and "Political Aspects of

Full Employment" facilitates the grasping of certain definite tendencies in contemporary capitalism. These tendencies are particularly pronounced in those countries which in a particular period play—or at least try to play—the role of saviors of the capitalist world.

The author shows the fallacy of identifying Nazism, with its economic background and political consequences, with "The Fascism of Our Times" (*Polityka,* 1964); but it would be as wrong to disassociate these two phenomena entirely, disregarding their common roots and the similar dangers they present. (The dangers are only qualitatively similar; quantitatively they must be increased in proportion to the progress of the technology of destruction.)

Reading this little volume may not always be easy for a layman. This applies especially to the paper "The Economic Situation in the United States as Compared with the Pre-War Period" (published in *Ekonomista* in 1956). It seems to me, however, that it is worth undertaking the effort to read the whole because only then will the character of the interrelations between economic analysis and political conclusions be clearly seen. Taking into consideration the work that Kalecki has done in the field of the dynamics of the capitalist economy, this is essential for appreciating the weight of these conclusions.

May 1967

Stimulating the Business Upswing in Nazi Germany (*1935*)

1. The stimulation of the business upswing in Germany in the last two years supplies empirical data essential for the understanding of economic processes. The mechanism of the upswing is in this case exceptionally clearcut. Since it is the government that finances investment by means of credit, it is easy to discern the cause and effect and analyze precisely the process of creating purchasing power.

Moreover, the German experiment clearly shows the limits of the business upswing in the area of balance of payments if this upswing is not accompanied by an influx of foreign capital. Finally, we may observe in Germany a specific process—one not devoid, however, of general significance—the process of using for armament purposes those results of the business upswing which should be reflected in the increased consumption of the broad masses of the population.

2. The general pattern of stimulating the business upswing in Germany was as follows: Central and local government agencies engaged in public investment and were

paid in "work supply bills" discounted in the banks by the various firms. In this way additional purchasing power was created, effective demand was increased, and production rose. Since the increase in money in circulation was rather small—most of the outlays returned to the banks as deposits or as repayments of credits—the amounts in question were at the disposal of the banks for further discounting of the "work supply bills" by which continuing public investment was financed. As a result, the indebtedness of the central and local government increased: either the bank deposits and bank holdings of "work supply bills" increased or these bills took the place of private exchange bills in the banks' portfolios. The latter caused a shift in the structure of bill holdings of the banking system from private to public bills, with a large part of the public bills finding their way to the Reichsbank and almost entirely filling its portfolio.

The formal term of all public bills was three months. In fact, however, these were long-term debts of the central and local government; the payment of bills actually consisted of issuing new ones. Some people expect that in some unspecified way such a situation will end in "bankruptcy." It is, however, difficult to fathom how this can happen if the Reichsbank does not refuse to discount the public bills—which is, to put it mildly, rather unlikely. The special advantage of long-term credit actually results from the fact that the debtor is not certain of the possibility of a continuing conversion of short-term liabilities. However, in this case such a certainty does exist and as a result commitments which are in essence long term may be financed by short-term credits. (It is true that the government itself took some steps to convert the short-term debt into a long-term one, but this operation made little progress and was dictated by different considerations, as, for instance, by the interests of private banks.)

It is worthwhile pondering the following. When it comes to the point that the portfolio of the Reichsbank contains only public bills—and, as noted, this situation is in sight —the amounts spent by the government can no longer return to the Reichsbank via repayment of credits by private firms, and therefore public bills must start accumulating at private banks. What will happen if these banks are unwilling to hold them? The proposed solution for such an emergency is as formal as the misgivings private banks have about holding the "work supply bills": the Reichsbank is to issue its own bills to be sold to private banks and the money is to be used for discounting public bills; in other words, the central bank is to rediscount the public bills in private banks. From this "bill" point of view no threat to the German stimulation of the upswing seems to be imminent. It involves a real danger, but one of a quite different nature which we shall discuss in due course.

3. The increase in profits which occurred in 1933 as a result of financing public investment by credit caused a considerable rise in investment in 1934. As will be seen from Table 1, private industrial investment "made good" 50 percent of the decline that had occurred during the crisis. This is not much less than the corresponding percentage for industrial production as a whole, which amounted to 60 percent.

However, residential construction, less closely connected to the current business situation, lagged considerably behind despite some stimulation by the government.

As far as industrial investment was concerned, it was undertaken mostly by existing enterprises, while the creation of new establishments was rather an exception. One

TABLE 1

Item	*1932 : 1934* *(1929 = 100)*		*Ratio of increase (1932–34) to decline (1929–32) in percent*
Industrial production	58	83	60
Investment in industry	33	67	50
Residential construction	33	56	35

Based on the data of the German Institute of Survey of Current Business.

reason for this is the monopolistic character of German industry, and this was reinforced by the Nazi prohibition of new investment in a number of industries.

As will be seen, private investment increased considerably as a result of the government-stimulated upswing, but it still did not reach the level at which it could "overtake" public investment. (In particular, as noted above, residential building lagged considerably behind.) It is very interesting that at present the government is not particularly keen on any further increase in private investment. The point is that because of the difficulties in securing an adequate supply of foreign raw materials—about which more will be said below—a further increase in production is inhibited. This prevents the continuation of the upswing, so that an increase in private investment would require a reduction in the credit financing of public investment. This reduction, however, is also an aim per se because of its being military or para-military in character. As a result, recent official pronouncements talk of securing for the government an "undiminished credit basis." We can observe the paradoxical misgivings about the stimulation of the upswing succeeding too well.

4. It is obvious that the upswing of business in Germany had to cause an increased demand for the goods which were not produced in that country at all, or not in sufficient quantities, such as food, industrial raw materials, etc. The resulting difficulties experienced by Germany are today generally known. They are well illustrated by Table 2.

It will be seen first of all that Germany succeeded in increasing the general volume of imports by only a small amount, even though it suspended the servicing of foreign debts, which is tantamount to securing an additional source of foreign exchange. This is accounted for by a continuing decline in the volume of exports, slightly overcompensated by the suspension of foreign transfers.

The shrinkage of German exports in the period considered resulted mainly from a decline in total imports of the main importers of German goods—the countries of Western and Middle Europe as well as the USSR—between 1932 and 1934. As far as the USSR is concerned, a fall in the Germans' relative share in its imports probably occurred for political reasons.

Import restrictions caused a significant increase in the prices of food, as imports declined. (See Table 2.) There was also a rise in the price of industrial goods with a high foreign raw material content as a result of an inadequate increase in their import. (Examples are textiles, products made from nonferrous metals, soap, etc.) The increase in prices, along with regulations prohibiting the use of raw materials for certain purposes (e.g., copper in building) led

TABLE 2

Item	*1932*	*1934* (*1929 = 100*)	*Ratio of increase (1932–34) to decline (1929–32) in percent*
Industrial production	58.0	83.0	60
Volume of imports	70.0	72.5	8
food	74.5	63.0	—
industrial raw materials and semi-manufactured goods	73.5	82.0	32
finished goods	50.0	59.5	19

Based on data of the German Institute of Survey of Current Business and the Government Statistical Office.

to a state of semi-autarky. This was reflected in a more intensive agriculture, the mining of poor ores, and the resorting to substitutes (aluminum in lieu of copper), to synthetic raw materials (artificial fiber, gasoline from coal), and to the use of second-hand goods and waste on a larger scale.

All this facilitated the rise in production in the face of an inadequate supply of foreign raw materials. It seems, however, that the relation of the former to the latter has been strained to the limit: without an increase in imports, which may be achieved merely by a rise in exports (since there is no chance of an influx of foreign capital), German production can hardly grow, and government intervention in the circumstances is confined to maintaining the current level of economic activity. We referred to this situation when in the preceding section we pointed to the competition between private investment and armaments. We shall see below that armaments also compete with consumption.

5. Let us now consider the question of the effect of the German business upswing on consumption. To what extent did the working class profit from the government's stimulation of this upswing? As will be seen from Table 3, the increase in consumption was totally incommensurate with that of industrial production: while from 1932 to 1933 60 percent of the decline in industrial production of the period 1929–1932 was "made good," in consumption the figure is only 28 percent. How can this disproportion be accounted for? Why was a considerable increase in employment so little reflected in the consumption of wage and salary earners?

TABLE 3

Item	*1932* (*1929 = 100*)	*1934* (*1929 = 100*)	*Ratio of increase (1932–34) to decline (1929–32) in percent*
Industrial production	58	83	60
Retail sales at constant prices	82	87	28

Based on data of the German Institute of the Survey of Current Business.

One of the reasons follows directly from the preceding section. The increase in prices of consumer goods—particularly food—in relation to wages as a result of import restrictions must have restrained consumption to some extent. However, this was not the only factor hampering the increase in consumption.

The business upswing in Germany naturally caused an increase in government revenue. As a result of the rise in employment, the payment of unemployment benefits also declined considerably. What happened to the surplus that was thus accruing to the government? It was to a great extent spent on armaments. If this surplus was used to increase the salaries of officials or to increase benefits for the remaining unemployed, it would find its way to the consumer goods market rather than to the armament industries. The same would occur if the additional government revenues failed to materialize as a result of tax reductions: in the case of taxes on wages and salaries, this would increase the money purchasing power of workers; in the case of indirect taxation, the costs of production would fall and prices of consumer goods would tend to decline.

It will be seen that a considerable part of the potential increase in the purchasing power of the broad masses of the population was allocated to armaments. It is true that a question arises here of what would have happened if this had not been the case, if there had not been an inadequate supply of foreign raw materials. Would not the increase in the purchasing power of consumers have then resulted in an additional rise in prices? Such would in fact be the case if armament production did not require foreign materials. This, however, is obviously not the case because this production does absorb large quantities of (mostly non-ferrous) metals which have lately been imported into Germany. Thus even in the present position of German foreign trade, consumption could have increased if materials for consumer goods industries had been imported instead of those for the manufacture of armaments.

The effects of the German business upswing in the field of consumption are of considerable interest from a more general point of view. The business upswing is always reflected in an increase in the degree of utilization of equipment. The German example shows that this need not necessarily be associated with a commensurate rise in the standard of living of the broad masses of the population.

Political Aspects of Full Employment (*1943*)

The maintenance of full employment through government spending financed by loans has been widely discussed in recent years. This discussion, however, has concentrated on the purely economic aspects of the problem without giving due consideration to political realities. The assumption that a government will maintain full employment in a capitalist economy if it only knows how to do it is fallacious. In this connection the misgivings of big business about the maintenance of full employment by government spending is of paramount importance. This attitude was shown clearly in the Great Depression in the 1930's, when big business consistently opposed experiments for increasing employment by government spending in all countries except Nazi Germany. The attitude is not easy to explain. Clearly, higher output and employment benefits not only workers but businessmen as well, because their profits rise. And the policy of full employment based on loan-financed government spending does not encroach upon profits because it does not involve any additional taxation. The businessmen in a slump are longing for a boom; why do they not accept gladly the "synthetic" boom which the government is able to offer them? It is this difficult and fascinating question we intend to deal with in this article.

I

1. The reasons for the opposition of the "industrial leaders" to full employment achieved by government spending may be subdivided into three categories: (a) the dislike of government interference in the problem of employment as such; (b) the dislike of the direction of government spending/public investment and subsidizing consumption; (c) the dislike of the social and political changes resulting from the *maintenance* of full employment. We shall examine each of these three categories of objections to the government expansion policy in detail.

2. We shall deal first with the reluctance of the "captains of industry" to accept government intervention in the matter of employment. Any widening of state activity is looked upon by "business" with suspicion, but the creation of employment by government spending has a special aspect which makes the opposition particularly intense. Under a *laissez-faire* system the level of employment depends to a great extent on the so-called state of confidence. If this deteriorates, private investment declines, which results in a fall of output and employment (both directly and through the secondary effect of the fall in incomes upon consumption and investment). This gives to the capitalists a powerful indirect control over government policy: everything which may shake the state of confidence must be carefully avoided because it would cause an economic crisis. But once the government learns the trick of increasing employment by its own purchases, this powerful control-

ling device loses its effectiveness. Hence budget deficits necessary to carry out government intervention must be regarded as perilous. The social function of the doctrine of "sound finance" is to make the level of employment dependent on the "state of confidence."

3. The dislike of the business leaders of a government spending policy grows even more acute when they come to consider the objects on which the money would be spent: public investment and subsidizing mass consumption.

The economic principles of government intervention require that public investment should be confined to objects which do not compete with the equipment of private business (e.g., hospitals, schools, highways, etc.). Otherwise the profitability of private investment might be impaired and the positive effect of public investment upon employment offset by the negative effect of the decline in private investment. This conception suits the businessmen very well. But the scope of public investment of this type is rather narrow, and there is a danger that the government, in pursuing this policy, may eventually be tempted to nationalize transport or public utilities so as to gain a new sphere in which to carry out investment.*

One might therefore expect business leaders and their experts to be more in favor of subsidizing mass consumption (by means of family allowances, subsidies to keep down the prices of necessities, etc.) than of public investment, for by subsidizing consumption the government would not be embarking on any sort of "enterprise." In

* It should be noted here that investment in a nationalized industry can contribute to the solution of the problem of unemployment only if it is undertaken on principles different from those of private enterprise. The government may have to be satisfied with a lower net rate of return than private enterprise and must deliberately time its investment so as to mitigate slumps.

practice, however, this is not the case. Indeed, subsidizing mass consumption is much more violently opposed by these "experts" than is public investment. For here a "moral" principle of the highest importance is at stake. The fundamentals of capitalist ethics require that "You shall earn your bread in sweat"—unless you happen to have private means.

4. We have considered the political reasons for the opposition against the policy of creating employment by government spending. But even if this opposition were overcome—as it may well be under the pressure of the masses—the *maintenance* of full employment would cause social and political changes which would give a new impetus to the opposition of the business leaders. Indeed, under a regime of permanent full employment, "the sack" would cease to play its role as a disciplinary measure. The social position of the boss would be undermined and the self-assurance and class consciousness of the working class would grow. Strikes for wage increases and improvements in conditions of work would create political tensions. It is true that profits would be higher under a regime of full employment than they are on the average under *laissez-faire;* and even the rise in wage rates resulting from the stronger bargaining power of the workers is less likely to reduce profits than to increase prices, and thus affects adversely only the rentier interests. But "discipline in the factories" and "political stability" are more appreciated by the business leaders than are profits. Their class instinct tells them that lasting full employment is unsound from their point of view and that unemployment is an integral part of the normal capitalist system.

II

1. One of the important functions of fascism, as typified by the Nazi system, was to remove the capitalist objections to full employment.

The dislike of government spending policy as such is overcome under fascism by the fact that the state machinery is under the direct control of a partnership of big business and fascist upstarts. The necessity for the myth of "sound finance," which served to prevent the government from offsetting a confidence crisis by spending, is removed. In a democracy one does not know what the next government will be like. Under fascism there is no next government.

The dislike of government spending, whether on public investment or consumption, is overcome by concentrating government expenditure on armaments. Finally, "discipline in the factories" and "political stability" under full employment are maintained by the "new order," which ranges from the suppression of the trade unions to the concentration camp. Political pressure replaces the economic pressure of unemployment.

2. The fact that armaments are the backbone of the policy of fascist full employment has a profound influence upon its economic character. Large-scale armaments are inseparable from the expansion of the armed forces and the preparation of plans for a war of conquest. They also induce competitive rearmament of other countries. This causes the main aim of the spending to shift gradually from full employment to securing the maximum effect of rearmament. The resulting scarcity of resources leads to the curtailment of consumption as compared with what it could have been under full employment.

The fascist system starts from the overcoming of unemployment, develops into an "armament economy" of scarcity, and ends inevitably in war.

III

1. What will be the practical outcome of the opposition to "full employment by government spending" in a capitalist democracy? We shall try to answer this question on the basis of the analysis of the reasons for this opposition given in section II. We argued that we may expect the opposition of the "leaders of industry" on three planes: (a) the opposition on principle against government spending based on a budget deficit; (b) the opposition against this spending being directed either toward public investment—which may foreshadow the intrusion of the state into the new spheres of economic activity—or toward subsidizing mass consumption; and (c) the opposition against *maintaining* full employment and not merely preventing deep and prolonged slumps.

Now, it must be recognized that the stage in which the "business leaders" could afford to be opposed to *any* kind of government intervention to alleviate a slump is rather a matter of the past. The necessity that "something must be done in the slump" is agreed to; but the conflict continues, first, as to what should be the direction of government intervention in the slump, and second, as to whether it should be used merely to alleviate slumps or to secure permanent full employment.

2. In the current discussions of these problems there emerges time and again the conception of counteracting the slump by stimulating *private* investment. This may be done by lowering the rate of interest, by reducing the corporate income tax, or by subsidizing private investment

directly in this or another form. That such a scheme should be attractive to "business" is not surprising. The businessman remains the medium through which the intervention is conducted. If he does not feel confidence in the political situation he will not be bribed into investment. And the intervention does not involve the government either in "playing with" (public) investment or "wasting money" on subsidizing consumption.

It may be shown, however, that the stimulation of private investment does not provide an adequate method for preventing mass unemployment. There are two alternatives to be considered here: (A) The rate of interest or corporate income tax (or both) is reduced sharply in the slump and increased in the boom. In this case both the period and the amplitude of the business cycle will be reduced, but employment not only in the slump but even in the boom may be far from full—i.e., the average unemployment may be considerable, although its fluctuations will be less marked. (B) The rate of interest or corporate income tax is reduced in a slump but *not* increased in the subsequent boom. In this case the boom will last longer but it must end in a new slump: one reduction in the rate of interest or corporate income tax does not, of course, eliminate the forces which cause cyclical fluctuations in a capitalist economy. In the new slump it will be necessary to reduce the rate of interest or corporate income tax again and so on. Thus in not too remote a time the rate of interest would have to be negative and corporate income tax would have to be replaced by an income subsidy. The same would arise if it were attempted to *maintain* full employment by stimulating private investment: the rate of interest and corporate income tax would have to be reduced continuously.

In addition to this fundamental weakness of combating

unemployment by stimulating private investment, there is a practical difficulty. The reaction of businessmen to the measures described is uncertain. If the downswing is sharp they may take a very pessimistic view of the future, and the reduction of the rate of interest or corporate income tax may then for a long time have little or no effect upon investment, and thus upon the level of output and employment.

3. Even those who advocate stimulating private investment to counteract the slump frequently do not rely on it exclusively but envisage that it should be associated with public investment. It looks at present as if "business leaders" and their experts (at least some of them) would tend to accept as a *pis aller* public expenditure financed by borrowing as a means of alleviating slumps. They seem, however, still to be consistently opposed to creating employment by subsidizing consumption and to *maintaining* full employment.

This state of affairs is perhaps symptomatic of the future economic regime of capitalist democracies. In the slump, either under the pressure of the masses, or even without it, public investment financed by borrowing will be undertaken to prevent large scale unemployment. But if attempts are made to apply this method in order to maintain the high level of employment reached in the subsequent boom, a strong opposition of "business leaders" is likely to be encountered. As has already been argued, lasting full employment is not at all to their liking. The workers would "get out of hand" and the "captains of industry" would be anxious to "teach them a lesson." Moreover, the price increase in the upswing is to the disadvantage of small and big rentiers and makes them "boom tired."

In this situation a powerful bloc is likely to be formed between big business and the rentier interests, and they would probably find more than one economist to declare that the situation was manifestly unsound. The pressure of all these forces, and in particular that of big business, would most probably induce the government to return to the orthodox policy of cutting down the budget deficit. A slump would follow, in which government spending policy would come again into its own.

This pattern of a "political business cycle" is not entirely conjectural; something very much like that happened in the United States in 1937–1938. The breakdown of the boom in the second half of 1937 was actually due to the drastic reduction of the budget deficit. On the other hand, in the acute slump that followed the government promptly reverted to a spending policy. Thus the regime of the "political business cycle" would not secure full employment except at the top of the boom, but slumps would be relatively mild and shortlived.

The Economic Situation in the United States as Compared with the Pre-War Period (*1956*)

I

From the last years of the inter-war period up to the present there were considerable changes in the volume and structure of the national product, in the degree of unemployment, and in the standard of living of the United States. This is illustrated by Table 1, based on official sources, where we compare the years 1937 and 1955. The top year of the business upswing following the great crisis was 1937; it represents about the same phase of the business cycle as 1955.

During the eighteen-year period considered the national product had more than doubled.* From the point of view of supply this increase may be easily explained; indeed, during this period—which covers the Second World War,

* We take the national product inclusive of depreciation but exclusive of administrative services (i.e., remuneration of the armed forces and government employees) and of net income from foreign investment. In other words, this is the private home-produced Gross National Product.

reconversion, and the new gigantic rearmament—capital equipment expanded considerably. The expansion of heavy industry in the course of the war was financed by the government. After the war the productive capacities thus created were sold at low prices to private big business. In the period of reconversion the "civilian" sector was renovated and expanded, actuated by the "deferred demand" for consumer goods (especially durable commodities) which resulted from the deficiency of such goods during the war, accompanied by an accumulation of liquid savings. Finally, in the last phase of the eighteen-year period considered a large part of investment was connected with armaments.

The growth of the national product was not hampered by a shortage of labor. First of all, output per person employed increased by nearly 60 percent. This, in addition to "normal" technical progress, was the result of a rapid expansion of capital equipment, which led to a "rejuvenation," as well as of a continuous drive to increase labor intensity. It should also be mentioned that there was a technical revolution in agriculture, as a concentration of farm ownership proceeded at a rapid pace. The resulting rate of increase in the productivity of labor meant that the supply of labor proved adequate for the large growth of the national product referred to above. This follows directly from the fact that in 1955 unemployment amounted to 4 percent of the labor force. (This includes the self-employed; if these were eliminated the unemployment percentage would prove even higher.)

The fact that as a result of specific situations associated with the war (no destruction was suffered) and with armaments there occurred a growth of productive potential which made it possible to double the national product still does not explain the effective utilization of these

TABLE 1

Item	*1937*	*1955*
Industrial and agricultural production	100	201.6
National product at 1947 prices	100	209.5
Personal consumption at 1947 prices	100	193.0
Relative share of personal consumption in national product	78.7%	72.5%
National product per person employed in its production*	100	158.5
Personal consumption per head of population	100	150.7
Unemployment in relation to total labor force	14.2%	3.8%

The figures in this table, as well as in tables 2, 3, and 4, are based on *National Income 1954* (a supplement to the *Survey of Current Business*), *Economic Report of the President 1956,* and *Survey of Current Business,* July 1956.

* Employment in the production of national product = labor force – unemployed, the armed forces, and government employees. Thus this item includes all self-employed.

facilities. Indeed, the discrepancy between the development of productive forces and the markets for their products constitutes one of the main contradictions inherent in the capitalist system.

In the period considered this contradiction tended to grow more acute. As we shall see below, big business's relative share of accumulation of the national product increased significantly—this may already be surmised from the decline of personal consumption in relation to national product in the period 1937–1955 shown in Table 1. It should be noticed that this is not an accident depending on the choice of the years compared: similar results are obtained for a few years preceding 1955 when compared with the second half of the prewar decade. Thus one question arises as to why this aggravation of basic contradictions did not lead to the underemployment of resources.

A second question concerns the increase of the standard of living compared with the rise in productivity and the decline in the percentage of unemployment. As seen in Table 1, consumption lags behind national product by 8 percent. The standard of living lags by not much less (5 percent) behind the national product per person employed in its production. But we might have expected a higher impact upon the standard of living from a considerable decline in the percentage of unemployment (from 14 to 4 percent).

In the rest of this paper we shall find that:

1. The increase of the relative share of big business's accumulation of the national product was absorbed by armaments (mainly through the tax on corporate profits and the export surplus, whose realization was also closely connected to the expenditures of the armament-imperialist complex).

2. The decline in unemployment was associated to a great extent with an increase in the armed forces and in government employees; as a result, the rise in the degree of employment did not have much effect on the standard of living, which increased mainly owing to a higher productivity of labor.

II

In order to analyze the effect of the increased relative share of accumulation in the national product we shall divide this product into three parts: (a) private accumulation, (b) "net revenue of the government* from persons," c) personal consumption of goods and services. We shall now explain in detail the nature of the first two and we shall prove that together with personal consumption they just cover the national product.

It should first be recalled that national product here means gross of depreciation. (By the way, depreciation in capitalist countries is determined by deductions permissible by fiscal rules and cannot therefore be a measure of actual capital consumption.) Accordingly, accumulation is considered to be inclusive of depreciation.

Gross accumulation consists of investment in fixed capital, which we break down into "productive investment," residential building, increase in inventories, and the export surplus. As far as private accumulation is concerned, the budget deficit should still be taken into consideration, because it means an increase in the government's indebtedness to the capitalists.† Finally, we also

---

* By government, we mean here central, state, and local authorities.

† By "budget deficit" we mean the actual budget deficit. The following items have been deducted from it: (1) "foreign economic assistance," which is included in export surplus (armament export is *not* deducted, since it is not included in that surplus); and (2) government expenditure on goods abroad which we did not include in imports (although expenditure on personnel abroad, mainly military, *is* included in imports as a counterpart to the respective item in personal consumption).

include in private accumulation the revenue from the corporate profits tax as accumulation ceded to the government.

Item (b) represents the budget revenue exclusive of taxes on corporate profits but only to the extent to which they are spent on business products. Thus this is a surplus of personal income tax, contributions to social insurance plans, and indirect taxes* over and above the expenditure on remuneration of the armed forces (inclusive of food and uniforms) and of government employees, on social insurance benefits, and on interest on the public debt. In short, this is "net government revenue from persons," inclusive of indirect taxes.

It is easy to prove on the basis of Table 2 that, as mentioned above, the items shown here cover the national product. Indeed, productive investment, residential building, increase in inventories, and export surplus add to gross accumulation for the economy as a whole. The budget deficit, taxes on corporate profits, and "net government revenue from persons" are all the sources which cover government expenditure on business products.† But gross social accumulation, government expenditure on business products, and personal consumption constitute the Gross National Product in our sense—the gross private home-produced national product.

In order to examine the changes in structure of the national product, Table 3 shows the items from Table 2 as a percent of national product.

* By indirect taxes we mean the actual revenue from this source minus subsidies for private businesses plus profits from government enterprises.

† The money value of these three components was deflated by a 1947 = 100 price index of the total government expenditure on business products.

TABLE 2

Item	1937 (in billion $ at 1947 prices)	1955
Productive investment	12.9	30.1
Residential building	3.9	12.9
Increase in inventories	5.7	3.7
Export surplus (+) or import surplus (—)	–0.7	3.7
Gross accumulation	21.8	50.4
Budget deficit (+) or surplus (—)	–1.3	–4.8
Taxes on corporate profits	2.7	17.2
Gross private accumulation	23.2	62.8
"Net government revenue from persons"	6.9	18.7
Personal consumption	111.9	216.0
National product	142.0	297.5

It will be seen at once that the most important change is the fall in the relative share of consumption in the national product, mainly associated with an increase in private gross accumulation and to a lesser extent with an increase in net government revenue from persons.

Let us analyze in more detail the increase in the relative share of gross private accumulation in the national

TABLE 3

Item	1937	1955
	(at 1947 prices and	
	in % of national product)	
Productive investment	9.1	10.1
Residential building	2.8	4.3
Increase in inventories	4.0	1.3
Export surplus (+) or import surplus (—)	-0.5	1.3
Gross accumulation	15.4	17.0
Budget deficit (+) or surplus (—)	-0.9	-1.6
Taxes on corporate profits	1.9	5.8
Gross private accumulation	16.4	21.2
"Net government revenue from persons"	4.9	6.3
Personal consumption	78.7	72.5
National product	100	100

product. It appears that this is more than accounted for by the increase of the relative share in the national product of two items: export surplus and taxes on corporate profits. It is easy to show that in either case we face the absorption of accumulation by the armament-imperialist complex.

The increased taxes on corporate profits finance the

armaments directly. As far as the rise in export surplus is concerned, it is partly accounted for by foreign economic assistance granted in exchange for political advantages. Another factor is government expenditure on business products abroad—such as building bases, etc.—which enables the countries concerned to earn dollars and thus to buy U.S. goods.*

If we add to this the fact that the increase in the relative share of gross private accumulation in the national product is the result of the increase in the accumulation of big business† we may sum up our analysis as follows:

The increase in the relative share of private accumulation in the national product resulting from the accumulation of big business did not cause any underemployment of productive resources for the following reasons: the additional private accumulation was absorbed by armaments and by the export surplus, whose increase was associated with "foreign economic assistance" or with the building of bases abroad which provided the wherewithal for importing American goods.

The increase in the relative share of private accumulation in the national product mainly accounted for the decline in the share of consumption. To a lesser extent this was caused by the increase in the relative share of "net

* This was not included in imports. See footnote, p. 89.

† In fact, the relative share of gross corporate accumulation in the national product increased more than that of total gross private accumulation. It was estimated that in 1937 the former amounted to about 0.4, and in 1955 to about 0.6, of the latter. It follows that gross corporate accumulation amounted to about 7 percent of the national product in 1937 and about 13 percent in 1955. The non-corporate gross private accumulation is that of dividend and interest receivers, of non-corporate entrepreneurs (including farmers), of higher business executives, and finally of the small savings of other wage and salary earners.

government revenue from persons." In this case a direct shift from consumption to armaments took place rather than the absorption of accumulation.*

III

In considering the reasons for the actual decline of the relative share of personal consumption in the national product of the United States we took into account only the *surplus* of personal tax revenue over transfers and the remuneration of soldiers and government employees, which are spent on consumer goods and services. Taxes used in this way do not reduce consumption but solely redistribute it to transfer recipients and to non-productive employees. The increase of the relative share of the latter in total employment alone accounts for the fact that the decline in the percentage of unemployment from 1937 to 1955 did not contribute much to the average standard of living. It appears that employment in the production of the private national product increased only a little more than did the total population. In fact, the decline in the unemployment percentage was to a great extent offset by the rise of the relative share of the armed forces and of government employees in the labor force (see Table 4).

Table 4 shows that the combined percentage of unemployed, armed forces, and government employees fell only slightly. Accordingly, the increase in the labor force lags only slightly behind that in employment in the production of the national product. Since the total population increased a trifle more than the labor force, this employment in relation to the former increased even less: by 3

* We say "rather" because in this case too there may take place to some extent an absorption of private accumulation.

TABLE 4

Item		*1937*	*1955*
Employment in production of national product		100	132.2
Labor force		100	126.8
Population		100	128.1
Unemployed	(*in percent of labor force*)	14.2	3.8
Armed forces and officials	(*in percent of labor force*)	7.5	14.5
Jointly		21.7	18.3

percent. It is clear now that the decline in unemployment was reflected only to a minor extent in the standard of living because it was associated with the relative shift from productive to non-productive employment—mainly as a consequence of militarization. As a result the increase in consumption per head of population lagged behind that of national product per person employed in its production almost as much as the increase in total consumption lagged behind that of the total national product (see Table 1).

IV

Let us ponder for a while on the results of our analysis. The militarization of the U. S. economy contributed to its high degree of utilization in two ways: First, the expenditures of the armament-imperialist complex on business products counteracted the disrupting influence of the increase in the relative share of accumulation of big business in the national product. Apart from this, the increase in the armed forces and in the number of government employees contributed to the reduction in unemployment. In both instances the potential increase in the standard of living was hampered; nevertheless, the actual increase was considerable because of the rise in productivity of labor.

It is clear that the *way* in which the reduction of unemployment and the relatively rapid increase in the standard of living was achieved point to the elements of decay in monopoly capitalism; but the actual consequences have a political impact which must not be underestimated. If we recall in addition that the mass communications media, such as the daily press, radio, and television, in the United States are largely under the control of the ruling class, the outline of the functioning of American imperialism will emerge clearly. It is based on the following "triangle":

1. Imperialism contributes to a relatively high level of employment through expenditures on armaments and ancillary purposes and through the maintenance of a large body of armed forces and government employees.

2. The mass communications media, working under the auspices of the ruling class, emits propaganda aimed at securing the support of the population for this armament-imperialist set-up.

3. The high level of employment and the standard of living increased considerably as compared with before the war (as a result of the rise in the productivity of labor), and this facilitated the absorption of this propaganda by the broad masses of the population.

This explains the fact that in the United States there is no significant opposition to armaments and the cold war; that the anti-capitalist undercurrent which characterized the New Deal period has slackened; and that the trade unions are part and parcel of the armament-imperialist set-up. Workers in the United States are not duller and trade union leaders are not more reactionary "by nature" than in other capitalist countries. Rather, the political situation in the United States is simply, in accordance with the precepts of historical materialism, the unavoidable consequence of economic developments and of characteristics of the superstructure of monopoly capitalism in its advanced stage.

The Fascism of Our Times (*1964*)

In the last few years we have noticed fervent activity among strong fascist groups in the developed capitalist countries. The most important of them are the OAS in France, the neo-Nazi elements in West Germany, and the Goldwaterites in the United States. All these groups have the following characteristics in common:

1. In contrast to the Nazism of the period of the great depression of the 1930's, they do not resort to social demagogy. Goldwaterism even espouses the reverse ideology by criticizing government intervention and proclaiming the return to *laissez-faire*.

2. They appeal to reactionary elements of the broad masses of the population by a variety of racist or chauvinistic slogans. For each of the countries considered these slogans can easily be condensed into one word: Algeria, revanche, Negroes. The fascist groups also proclaim the anti-communist crusade by capitalizing on a long period of official propaganda.

3. The fascist elements are subsidized by the most reac-

tionary groups of big business, which in this way usually also further their particular interests—the defense of their investments in Algeria, the expansion of certain branches of the armament industries, etc. The fascists are also súpported by certain groups in the armed forces.

4. However, the ruling class as a whole, even though it does not cherish the idea of fascist groups seizing power, does not make any effort to suppress them and confines itself to reprimands for overzealousness.

We shall try to examine these characteristics of contemporary fascism point by point below and in this way to put them into proper perspective.

I

One of the basic functions of Nazism was to overcome the reluctance of big business to large-scale government economic intervention. German big business agreed to a deviation from the principles of *laissez-faire* and to a radical increase of the role of the government in the national economy—on condition that the government machine would submit to direct control in their partnership with the Nazi leaders. However, the purely capitalist mode of production was guaranteed by directing the increased government expenditures to armaments rather than to productive investment (which would signify some bias toward state capitalism).

Today government economic intervention has become an integral part of "reformed" capitalism. In a sense the price of this reform was the Second World War and the Nazi genocide which were the final effect of the heavy rearmament that initially played the role of stimulating the business upswing.

Thus fascism is no longer the necessary basis of a system

of government intervention. It cannot proclaim the slogan of elimination of mass unemployment because in developed capitalist countries employment is maintained at a rather high level. On the contrary, Barry Goldwater, while exhibiting racist and cold war demagogy, about which more will be said below, attacks not only government "interference" in the economy but even social insurance. It is in this way that the support of the most reactionary business groups is paid for. And this is also the reason why he has no chance of seizing power. (It is interesting that in the pre-election polls even in the Southern states twice as many people favored Democrats over Republicans in the matter of maintaining prosperity.)

What all the present-day fascist currents have in common with Nazism is the anti-trade-union attitude, which again reflects the link with the reactionary big business groups. This will be discussed in more detail below.

II

Who makes up the mass basis of the fascist movement? Goldwater won 40 percent of the votes; and although the Republicans suffered a crushing defeat, Goldwater achieved a tremendous success.

In each of the countries considered a different part of the population yields, according to specific conditions, to a different slogan—each of which, however, is racist or chauvinistic in character. In the case of France those who yielded included the Algerian Frenchmen and those in the metropolis who were antagonistic toward the numerous Algerian immigrants. In West Germany the former Nazis, with quite a few things to hide in their pasts, are the right candidates; they are interested in embellishing Hitlerism, and this links up nicely with the revanchist ideology proclaimed in a somewhat milder form by the government. The resettlers who did not arrange their affairs to their full satisfaction (definitely a minority) are another group susceptible to neo-Nazism. Finally, in the United States the opponents of the Negro emancipation drive provide recruits for the reactionary groups considered; and this includes not only the Southern racists but all those hostile to Negro aspirations for jobs at present available only to whites.

In addition, in all cases the fascist ranks are reinforced by anti-communist fanatics who are the product of prolonged propaganda spread through the mass communications media.

The analogy between France and the United States is worth noticing here: in either case the main driving force of the fascist movement is the potential emancipation of the oppressed nations, or decolonization in the broad sense. The German variety of fascism is different, although even in this case the *Herrenvolk* notion can be found at its roots.

III

Information about the capitalist groups supporting the fascist currents is, of course, very incomplete. In France these no doubt included groups which had heavily invested in Algeria, although they were certainly not the only OAS sympathizers.

In the United States the oil interests in Texas, the armament industries of the West, and the Bank of America, also very active there, are some of the main groups. All are "young," "dynamic" concerns. They are not particularly worried about slumps because they think that not only will they survive them but that they will increase their possessions at the expense of "old" capitalist groups. At the same time the oil men of Texas are afraid of losing the special tax privileges they enjoy, and the armament industries are afraid of a slackening of the cold war—hence their dislike of government intervention and of the doctrine of coexistence.

It should be noted that these capitalist groups are much less "experienced" than the old rulers of the United States who, after a period of opposition to the New Deal, finally understood the inadequacies of *laissez-faire* capitalism. And last but not least: the political power of the "upstarts" does not at present correspond to their financial weight and so they are striving to create a government in which they will be the controlling stockholders.

It is they who permeate their political agents, like Goldwater, with the spirit of resistance against government intervention, including social insurance. They are the "youngest" of the capitalist oligarchy and paradoxically just for this reason the most anachronistic group. They cannot win but they do not lose either as they perform, together with their hirelings, a definite function in present-day capitalism.

The fascist groups have one other important "protector." These are the "angry" members of the military establishment who love the game of balancing on the brink of a precipice—if not on that of a preventive war. They are in a sense the counterpart of the "predatory" business groups and are frequently linked together. It is probable, however, that the weight of the "angry" members of the armed forces is greater than that of the "predatory" groups in the ruling class.

IV

It would be a very crude simplification to maintain that only the "upstarts" or some other specific groups of big business support the fascist movements. The boundaries are by no means so sharply drawn. It is very likely that many concerns financially support the official politicians of the ruling class as well as the less respectable adherents of fascism. This in turn is only one aspect of a broader phenomenon: the majority of the ruling class does not like the idea of the fascists seizing power, but at the same time it does not wish to crush them. The fascism of our times is a dog on a leash; it can be unleashed at any time to achieve definite aims and even when on the leash serves to intimidate the potential opposition.

Let us recall in this connection the role in the Algerian war of the OAS, that illegal terrorist organization which had "insiders" in all government offices and which was by no means persecuted by the government—indeed, it had its uses as a whip against the Algerian rebels and the internal opposition to the war. After the conclusion of the Evian agreement, OAS activity naturally slackened since the Frenchmen in Algeria were already powerless and the repatriates were settled in France under very favorable conditions. But OAS adherents probably managed to survive in the Gaullist party and the government establishment, especially in the armed forces. The threat of this alternative to the present government has some impact upon the present political situation: the government may be understood as keeping a bad dog on a leash.

A similar duality will be seen in West Germany. Even though the government disclaims any affinity whatever to Nazism and even though trials of war criminals take place from time to time, former Nazis who have hardly been "re-educated" occupy important administrative posts, especially in the armed forces. In the propaganda of revanche the fascist groups display, as said above, much more extreme views than the representatives of the government, who by no means find them embarrassing. At the same time the dog on the leash, which is fairly long, makes itself useful by extinguishing any glimpse of resistance to the official policy of cold war, revanche, and militarism.

An analogous phenomenon may be observed in the United States. It seems fairly certain that after the murder of John Kennedy the government would have been able to deal a mortal blow to the right-wing extremists. But the way of conducting the inquiry, as presented in the Warren Commission report, shows the contrary tendency to evade implicating anyone but Oswald—who in the meantime has been successfully eliminated. It is in this state of lawlessness that the origin of Goldwater's candidacy may be found. In turn, this candidacy was not very firmly opposed inside the Republican Party, as it was directly controlled by big business. The behavior of Eisenhower, who never tended to right-wing extremism, is quite significant here.

Goldwater is right, at least in a sense that this is not the end of his career. For Goldwaterism is wanted by the ruling class as a pressure group against an excessive relaxation of international tensions and in order to restrain the Negro movement. Goldwater will exist not only because of the support of the "predatory" groups of big business and the "angry" elements of the military machine, as well as of his racist and reactionary followers, but most of all because he will be saved by those to whom he lost.

Vietnam and U. S. Big Business (*1967*)

1. The last sentence of "The Facism of Our Times," written more than two years ago, was as follows: "Goldwater will exist not only because of the support of the 'predatory' groups of big business and the 'angry' elements of the military machine, as well as of his racist and reactionary followers, but most of all because he will be saved by those to whom he lost." This anticipation, which at that time might have seemed to some too pessimistic, appears in the perspective of the war in Vietnam rather too mild. It is true that not much is heard any longer of Goldwater, himself, but his spirit coexists in the White House.

It would be wrong, however, to shift to the other extreme and to maintain that the Johnson administration carries out all the postulates of Goldwaterism and thus represents the views and interests of the business groups which support it. There has been, indeed, no change in the government's attitude toward social insurance, trade unions, and the principles of government economic intervention. But the aggression in Vietnam, with its repercussions upon the armament industry (especially on the West Coast), is fully satisfactory to Goldwater and his masters.

It seems that at least until quite recently Johnson represented sort of a synthesis of the interests of all the big business groups. Indeed, the slogan of fighting the revolutionary movements in underdeveloped countries is shared by all these groups, and none of them objects to resorting to the most ruthless methods. At the same time, it was not until the middle of 1966, as we shall see in a while, that the economic repercussions of the war in Vietnam contributed to a weakening of the position of "old" big business—usually associated with the East Coast—in relation to such new "empires" as the Western and Southern armaments industry, the Bank of America, or the oilmen of Texas.

2. When writing about the war in Vietnam people refer frequently to the *total* U. S. military expenditure. In fact the gigantic level of this expenditure can be traced back to 1951; since then it has been an integral element of the U. S. economy. However, the increase in this expenditure up to the middle of 1966 was rather moderate. In the years 1964 and 1965 military expenditure on business products and personnel was maintained at a level of about $50 billion per year; in the first half of 1966 it amounted to $54 billion per year (after an approximate adjustment for the rise in prices). Moreover, even this moderate increase was not a fiscal business stimulant because the rise in public expenditure was offset by the hampering of consumption resulting from higher tax revenues.

The motive force of the boom in this period was in fact the increase in private investment (exclusive of residential building): from $61 billion in 1964 to $69 billion in 1965 to $75 billion in the first half of 1966 (all in 1964 prices). This was the result of earlier tax concessions of a type stimulating business investment and large orders—but not yet actual expenditures—in connection with the war in Vietnam. It is this increase in private investment which, together with its effects on consumption through higher employment and wages, led to the expansion of the Gross National Product:* from $632 billion in 1964 to $669 billion in 1965 to $699 billion in the first half of 1966 (in 1964 prices).

It follows from the above that: (a) the increase in military expenditure was not large in relation to the increase in national product and could not therefore lead to a major shift in the division of profits from "old" to "new" big businesses; and that (b) the war in Vietnam stimulated a business upswing by way of the impact of armament orders upon investment.

3. In the second half of 1966 the economic situation in the United States underwent a fundamental change. Military expenditures jumped from an annual rate of $54 billion in the first half of 1966 to $59 billion in the third quarter of that year (in 1964 prices). This very large increase, considering the short period in question, is probably accounted for by the investment in the armament industry having created the appropriate productive potential; this made it possible to increase the output in branches working up to capacity (e.g., in the production of bombers).

At the same time the private investment boom slackened and in residential building, which since 1964 had just managed to maintain its level, there was even a decline. It

* This is Gross National Product in the sense of official statistics: in contrast with the chapter "The Economic Situation in the United States as Compared with the Pre-War Period," neither net income from foreign investment nor administrative services (i.e., remuneration of armed forces and government employees) are deducted.

is military expenditures that now become the motive force of the business upswing as they increase, more than the hampering effect of tax revenue upon consumption. The Gross National Product increased from an annual rate of $699 billion in the first half to $708 billion in the third quarter of 1966 (in 1964 prices).

The situation is thus quite different from that prior to this period. The increase in military expenditure constitutes one-half of the increase of the national product; as a result, there appears a tendency for redistribution of national income to the armaments industries. Military expenditures begin to play a role as a business stimulant. To sum up: a typical war (or semi-war) boom started only in the second half of 1966.

To complete the picture it should be added that despite the increase in the cost of living the real wage bill from 1964 to the third quarter of 1966 rose at a rate of nearly 6 percent per year. This rapid rise was associated with increases both in employment and in real wages.

4. It is probable that military expenditures will continue to mount. This will change the distribution of profits to the advantage of the armaments industries, as well as reinforce the importance of armaments expenditures as a factor in the general economic situation. This in turn will no doubt strengthen the economic and political position of the "new" business groups. Their close association with the adventurous elements of the military machine will also contribute to such a shift in the structure of the ruling class.

Other factors will work in the same direction: a further expansion of the war will be accompanied by an ever increasing disregard for world opinion. This will adversely affect civil liberties, in particular the Negro problem, where the opinion of newly created African states has been a factor of considerable importance. The United States will drift toward membership in the club of "shameless countries," now including South Africa, Rhodesia, and Portugal. This will lead to the promotion in public life of reactionary politicians associated with "predatory" big business groups.

It is these groups that are the beneficiaries of the war in Vietnam and it is they that are interested in its continuation. At the same time the war will enhance their importance and this will in turn facilitate their pressure for its continuation.

The growing influence of armaments expenditures will work on the economic situation in the same way: the higher this expenditure, the more difficult the return to its former level—huge though it was—without causing a crisis. (Purely theoretically, this could be done by increasing other public expenditures or reducing taxes; in practice such a shift encounters serious difficulties because of the different interests and ideas among various big business groups.)

5. In the light of the above argument the "old" business groups should have serious misgivings about the continuation of the war in Vietnam: what is advantageous to their competitors undermines their own economic and political position in the ruling class.

Nor is this the end of the story. What they had in common with their adversaries—the effort to show the hopelessness of revolutionary movements in underdeveloped countries—has failed miserably. In this sense the war in Vietnam has already been lost. Indeed, the present impasse in the struggle of the country having the highest industrial potential—and one of two highest military potentials—against a revolutionary movement in a small underdeveloped country and against its similar socialist neighbor is nothing to boast about (even if the assistance of the Soviet Union to North Vietnam is taken into account). And in addition the ruling classes in the areas of potential future revolutions will not necessarily aspire to the "glorious" role of General Ky and in the light of Saigon's experience will not be particularly keen to call for U. S. assistance.

Finally, the more enlightened part of the U. S. ruling elite cannot help but see the rapid decline of American influence in Europe; this is most visible in French foreign policy but is by no means confined to it. This aspect of the war in Vietnam is particularly important for the "old" groups of big business because they are linked to Europe by their heavy investment there.

It follows from the above that the "old" groups of American big business have many reasons for not being enthusiastic about the war in Vietnam. The most reactionary elements of these groups "dream" about cutting it short (for instance, by means of nuclear bombing; however, that might, to put it mildly, involve some undesirable "complications"). The more reasonable may be inclined to withdraw from this hideous and misfired adventure.

This, regrettably, seems to be the only way to peace. It is difficult to expect any pressure in this direction on the part of organized workers in the near future. The most important factor here is the steady rise in employment and real wages since 1964 mentioned above. The central trade union organization, the AFL-CIO, whose bargaining position is reinforced by this development, has never uttered any objection to the war in Vietnam which would stimulate protests against it among its rank and file. Only a few left-wing trade unions, which do not belong to this central organization, have taken a different attitude.

It is true that various groups of intellectuals, in particular professors and students, have reacted strongly against the war in Vietnam. These, however, are a rather thin stratum of society in the United States without much political weight. It is possible that this "awakening" of the intelligentsia is important for U. S. political developments in the longer run, but it cannot have a major significance for stopping the war in Vietnam.

6. But is it possible that the groups of "old" big business associated with the East coast might play a role in the war in Vietnam comparable to that de Gaulle played in terminating the Algerian war? We have so far argued only that following this pattern would correspond to the basic interests of this group. Is there, however, any sign of a tendency to undertake such an action?

There is only one phenomenon, I think, pointing in this direction: the great number of publications in the United States since autumn 1966 on the subject of the murder of Kennedy. It is remarkable that these did not begin to appear until two years after the report of the Warren Commission and just at the time that, as said above, the war began to play a decisive part in the economic situation. During the preceding two years there had been no lack of books and articles criticizing the official version of Kennedy's death, but the books did not find publishers and were printed abroad, and the articles only appeared in periodicals with small circulations. The daily press and the leading weeklies accepted without reservation the verdict of the Warren Commission. Now the situation has changed. Books are being published and articles are appearing in such weeklies as *Look* or the *Saturday Evening Post* (associated with big business on the East coast) which not only criticize the conduct of the inquiry into the murder of Kennedy but even demand that it be reopened.

Well, it may be asked, how does this link up with the war in Vietnam? The point is that the United States is so deeply involved in it that the big businesses which embarked upon large-scale investment in connection with this war will be so desperately insisting on its continuation that it will require quite an upheaval to bring it to an end. The role of such an upheaval might be performed by the reopening of an inquiry into the murder of Kennedy—on the condition, of course, that it would not use the methods of the Warren Commission. Such an inquiry might establish the links between the "predatory" groups of big business and the scheme for the murder of Kennedy and thus compromise the present administration. In the atmosphere of this terrific scandal it might be possible to achieve the acceptance of the U Thant appeal for stopping the bombing of North Vietnam, for an armistice in South Vietnam, and for a start of negotiations with the Vietcong.

It is a sad world indeed where the fate of all mankind depends upon the fight between two competing groups within American big business. This, however, is not quite new: many far-reaching upheavals in human history started from a cleavage at the top of the ruling class.

Intermediate Regimes (*1966*)

1. History has shown that lower-middle-class and rich peasantry are rather unlikely to perform the role of the ruling class. Whenever social upheavals did enable representatives of these classes to rise to power, they invariably served the interests of big business (often allied with the remnants of the feudal system). This despite the fact that there is a basic contradiction between the interests of the lower middle class and big business—to mention only one: the displacement of small firms by business concerns.

Are there any specific conditions today favoring the emergence of governments representing the interests of the lower middle class (including in this the corresponding strata of the peasantry)? It would seem that such conditions do arise at present in many underdeveloped countries:

(a) At the time of achieving independence the lower middle class is very numerous while big business is predominantly foreign controlled with a rather small participation of native capitalists.

(b) Patterns of government economic activity are now

widespread. Apart from the obvious case of socialist countries, state economic intervention plays an important role in developed capitalist countries.

(c) It is also possible to obtain foreign capital through credits granted by socialist countries.

2. In the process of political emancipation—especially if this is not accompanied by armed struggle—representatives of the lower-middle-class rise to power in a natural way.

To keep in power they must: (a) achieve not only political but also economic emancipation, i.e., gain a measure of independence from foreign capital; (b) carry out land reform; and (c) assure continuous economic growth—this last point is closely connected with the other two.

By endeavoring at least to limit foreign influence, the lower-middle-class government heads into conflict with the "comprador" elements. When carrying out land reform it clashes with the feudal landlords. However, it may not necessarily be inclined to defy the native upper middle class. Reliance on this class in the strategy of economic development could easily result in the repetition of a well-known historical pattern—the final submission of the lower middle class to the interests of big business. This, however, is prevented by the weakness of the native upper middle class and its inability to perform the role of "dynamic entrepreneur" on a large scale. The basic investment for economic development must therefore be carried out by the state, which leads directly to a pattern of amalgamation of the interests of the lower middle class with state capitalism.

The realization of this pattern is facilitated by the participation of the state in the management of the economy, a phenomenon characteristic of our era. A large part of the world population today lives in the centrally planned socialist economies. But in the developed capitalist countries today a fair measure of state interventionism also prevails, and at the very least it is aimed at preventing business downswings. We are all "planners" today, although very different in character. No wonder, then, that the underdeveloped countries, striving to expand their economic potential as fast as possible (while the main concern of the developed capitalist countries is to utilize fully available productive capacities) tend to draw up plans of economic development. The next step is to provide for a large volume of investment in the public sector, since, as shown by experience, the private initiative cannot be relied upon to undertake an adequate volume of investment of appropriate structure. Thus state capitalism is closely connected with planning of one form or another which underdeveloped countries can hardly avoid today.

Evolution in this direction could be counteracted significantly by the pressure of the imperialist countries, exerted by attaching appropriate "strings" to credits granted. Since underdeveloped countries cannot do without some inflow of foreign capital, pressure of this kind could be highly effective in changing the lower-middle-class governments into servile tools of big business allied with the feudal class. Apart from an "ideological" victory, imperialist countries would gain a better foothold for defending their "old" investments in underdeveloped countries and for a "new" expansion in this sphere. A significant obstacle to these imperialist pressures, though, is the possibility of obtaining credits from socialist countries. Its effect is reflected not merely in the amount of capital actually received from this source by underdeveloped countries, but also in strengthening their bargaining position in dealing with the financial capitalist powers. The competition with the socialist countries for influence in the "intermediate regimes" forces those powers to grant credits without attaching conditions as to the internal economic policy, although the imperialist governments do try to obtain as much as possible in this respect.

3. The social system in which the lower middle class cooperates with state capitalism calls for a somewhat more detailed discussion. To be sure, this system is highly advantageous to the lower middle class and the rich peasants; state capitalism concentrates investment on the expansion of the productive potential of the country. There is thus no danger of forcing the small firms out of business, which is a characteristic feature of the early stage of industrialization under *laissez-faire*. Next, the rapid development of state enterprises creates executive and technical openings for ambitious young men of the numerous ruling class. Finally, land reform, which is not preceded by an agrarian revolution, is conducted in such a way that the middle class which directly exploits the poor peasants—i.e., the moneylenders and merchants—maintains its position, while the rich peasantry achieves considerable gains in the process.

The antagonists of the ruling class are: from above, the upper middle class allied with foreign capital and the feudal landowners; from below, the small land-holders and landless peasants, as well as the poor urban population—workers in small factories and the unemployed or casually employed, mainly migrants from the countryside in search of a source of livelihood. On the other hand, white collar workers and the not very numerous workers in large establishments—who in underdeveloped countries are in a privileged position as compared with the urban and rural paupers—are frequently, especially when employed in state enterprises, allies of the lower middle class rather than its antagonists.

4. As to the antagonistic "higher" classes, the feudals are

generally deprived of political significance by land reform. They might retain parts of their land through fictitious sales to relatives (so as to evade the ceiling) but this does not put them in a strong position in the political and social life of the country. On the other hand, the relation to the upper middle class may range from far-reaching nationalization (usually with compensation) to a mere limitation of the scope of private investment coupled with attempts, as a rule rather ineffective, to adjust its structure to the general goals of development.

The political importance of big business in the country corresponds to these variants. In any case its tendency to oppose the government is checked by the fear of the urban and rural proletariat, from which it is effectively separated by the ruling lower middle class. The choice of the particular way of dealing with big business is determined not so much by the ideology of the ruling class as by the strength of big business. Without taking into consideration the existing economic conditions, one might expect more "socialism" from a Nehru than from a Nasser. It was, however, the other way around, because at the time of gaining political independence big business in India was much stronger than in Egypt.

5. Potentially at least, the urban and rural paupers are antagonistic toward the ruling class since they do not benefit from the change of social system such as described above, and profit relatively little from economic development. Land reform is conducted in such a way that a major share of the available land goes to the rich and medium-rich peasants while the small land-holders and the rural proletariat receive only very little land. Insufficient effort is made to free the poor peasantry from the clutches of money-lenders and merchants and to raise the wages of farm laborers. The resulting agrarian situation is one of

the factors limiting agricultural output within the general economic development since under the prevailing agrarian relations the small farms are unable to expand their production. The same is true of larger farms cultivated by tenants. The lagging of agriculture behind general economic growth leads to an inadequate supply of foodstuffs and an increase in their prices, which is again to the disadvantage of the "stepsons" of the system. Even if the aggregate real incomes of those strata do not decline as a result of the increase in employment, they do not show any appreciable growth.

Though the poorest strata of the society thus have no reason to be happy, they do not, for the time being at least, constitute a danger for the present system. The poor peasantry and rural proletariat are controlled by some form of a local oligarchy comprised of the petty bourgeoisie (merchants and money-lenders), the richer peasants, and the smaller landlords. The urban population without stable employment, and even domestic workers and workers in small factories, are not too dangerous either, because they are permanently threatened by unemployment and are difficult to organize.

In this context one can easily understand the repressions against the communists observable in a number of "intermediate regimes." This is not a question of competition between parallel ideologies; the communists are simply at least potential spokesmen for the rural and urban paupers, and the lower middle class is quite rightly afraid of the political activization of the latter.

It is true that this lower middle class and the prosperous peasants are not really rich; in many instances their standard of living is lower than that of workers in developed countries. But in comparison to the masses of poor peasants, who also flood the cities as unemployed or badly paid domestic workers, the petty bourgeois is a tycoon with a lot to lose. In this context it is no coincidence either that the governments in question favor religion—even to the point of adopting an official religion—and show a tendency toward the external expansion and militarism associated with it.

6. On the international scene, the internal position of the ruling lower middle class finds its counterpart in the policy of neutrality between the two blocs: an alliance with any of the blocs would strengthen the corresponding antagonist at home. At the same time the neutrality is very important in the context of foreign credits mentioned above.

The "intermediate regimes" are the proverbial clever calves that suck two cows: each bloc gives them financial aid in competition with the other. Thus has the "miracle" of getting out of the United States some credits with no strings attached as to internal economic policy been made possible.

It should be still noticed that foreign credits are of great importance to the "intermediate regimes." The lagging of their agriculture behind their overall development—caused to a great extent by institutional factors—results in a shortage of foodstuffs which the state covers partly by imports (since the paupers must not be pushed to the extremes). This creates additional difficulties in the already strained balance of payments for which the remedy is sought in foreign credits.

Such a position in international relations defends the "intermediate regimes," as said above, against the pressure from imperialist powers aimed at restoration of the "normal" rule of big business in which the foreign capital would play an appreciable role (though more limited than in the past). Without such external pressures it is highly unlikely that the amalgamation of the lower middle class with state capitalism would be destroyed and the classical capitalism reinstated.

The above was published in the bulletin of the Center for Research on Underdeveloped Countries, Warsaw, at the end of 1964. Although at that time Indonesia did not contradict the pattern of "intermediate regimes" we outlined, it was by no means its representative example and this for the following reasons:

1. In economic policy Indonesia lagged considerably behind a typical "intermediate regime." Agrarian reform was in actual fact fairly ineffective and changed relatively little in Indonesian agrarian conditions. Nor did the government make any consistent effort in terms of industrialization and planning; in particular a violent inflation was permitted to develop. More than that, the government made a point of granting priority to "national integration" (including the claims of West Irian and Northern Borneo) over economic and social problems.

2. On the other hand, Indonesian foreign policy was more anti-imperialist and anti-colonialist than that of other "intermediate regimes." This radicalism was partly associated with the territorial claims mentioned above (in particular with "confrontation with Malaysia"), but was definitely general in character.

3. The by-product of the fight for incorporation of West Iran and of the "confrontation with Malaysia" was the expansion of the army—which imposed a considerable burden on the economy—and the enhancing of the political power of its higher echelons.

4. As contrasted with other "intermediate regimes," Indonesia had a very large Communist Party. It was rooted

mainly in the dissatisfaction of the poor peasants and farm laborers. However, it cooperated with the regime on the basis of support for its anti-imperialist policies without militating strongly against its neglect of domestic economic and social problems and without being prepared for a showdown with the reactionary middle classes associated closely with the army. It is obvious that the Communist Party represented here a much greater threat to these classes than in other "intermediate regimes"; it was, however, still potential rather than actual.

It is the situation outlined above that created the basis for subsequent developments in Indonesia. The full history of the events of September 30, 1965, has not yet been written. It is clear at least that the Communists did not attempt a takeover and that in fact these events played the role of a *Reichstagsfeuer*. The anti-Communist terror that followed was unprecedented even in the history of counter-revolutions: in the space of a few months about 400,000 people were murdered. The army's higher echelons, representing largely the reactionary middle class and the rich peasants or even the semi-feudal elements, thus eliminated the "anomaly" of a powerful Communist part in an intermediate regime.

Also, the foreign policy swung back to "normal." Although as said above the army derived a great measure of its power from the policy of "confrontation with Malaysia," it has itself now terminated this policy. In general the radicalism of Indonesian foreign policy is over, although, at least for the time being, the non-alignment policy has not been abolished.

The economic problems which are emphasized by the new government are being blamed on its predecessors. However, the conclusions drawn from the catastrophic economic situation do not point at all to more planning or agrarian reform. The terror that rages not only against Communists but against radicals in general is probably considered an adequate substitute for progressive economic and social policies.